FiVE UNEASY PiECES

FIVE UNEASY PIECES

American Ethics in a Globalized World

Mark Gibney

ROWMAN & LITTLEFIELD PUBLISHERS, INC.
Lanham • Boulder • New York • Toronto • Oxford

ROWMAN & LITTLEFIELD PUBLISHERS, INC.

Published in the United States of America
by Rowman & Littlefield Publishers, Inc.
A wholly owned subsidiary of The Rowman & Littlefield Publishing
Group, Inc.
4501 Forbes Boulevard, Suite 200, Lanham, MD 20706
www.rowmanlittlefield.com

P.O. Box 317, Oxford OX2 9RU, UK

British Library Cataloguing in Publication Information Available

Library of Congress Cataloging-in-Publication Data

Gibney, Mark.
Five uneasy pieces : American ethics in a globalized world / Mark Gibney
    p.   cm.
   Includes bibliographical references and index.
   0-7425-3588-6 (cloth : alk. paper) — 0-7425-3589-4 (pbk. : alk. paper)
   1. Ethics—United States. 2. United States—Foreign relations—Moral
and ethical aspects.   3. United States—Foreign economic relations—
Moral and ethical aspects.   4. United States—Moral conditions.   I. Title.
JZ1480 .G53 2004
172'.4'0973—dc22   2004005881

Printed in the United States of America

♾ ™The paper used in this publication meets the minimum requirements
of American National Standard for Information Sciences—Permanence of
Paper for Printed Library Materials, ANSI/NISO Z39.48-1992.

CONTENTS

PREFACE

Since September 11, 2001, two questions have faced the American people: The first is, why was the United States attacked? The second is, how should the United States respond to being attacked? Both questions relate to America's place in the world.

This book is about America's place in the world; only it does not involve itself so much with geopolitical issues as with ethical issues. The book provides an analysis of how ethical (or unethical) America's actions in the world have been, but more than that, it examines the ethical framework that American society uses in our dealings with people outside the United States or those whom I will commonly refer to as "others." To summarize the pages that follow, notwithstanding a near obsession with "ethics" or "morality," the American people and the United States have displayed a very queer sense of ethics. Not only have many of our actions in the world been harmful, selfish, hypocritical, and rife with missed opportunities to do "good," but the ethical system that we have devised for ourselves has actually given us license to act this way. In short, in the name of ethics and under the guise of ethics, we have acted rather unethically.

Yet, within the past few years there have been some strong indications that our society has been in the midst of an ethical transformation. For one thing, the U.S. government (on behalf of the American people) has been willing to acknowledge and apologize for some of the horrible things that our country has done in the past. Beyond this, there are signs that our nation's ethical framework has broadened considerably so that millions of desperately sick and destitute people in faraway lands who never were a part of our ethical framework now are.

Then the events of September 11, 2001, came crashing down on us. The U.S. response was a war to remove the Taliban from power in Afghanistan, followed by a war against the Saddam Hussein regime in Iraq. Without question, various aspects of the "war on terrorism" contain elements of our old ethics, which is to say that in some ways the American people have reverted to a vision of the world that is divided between "us" and "them"— essentially all of them. Immediately, upward of two thousand men of Middle Eastern heritage were swept up and detained with very little judicial oversight or public outrage. Refugee numbers have plummeted. Civil liberties, generally, have been curtailed significantly. But beyond that, there are disturbing indications that, once more, the sole concern of the American people is America's self-interest.

On the other hand, there have been some encouraging developments in the post–September 11 period that indicate just the opposite, and that the ethical metamorphosis of the American people is in some ways continuing. For the first time in a decade, U.S. foreign aid has been increased—and increased rather substantially—although the amounts are still far too small and nowhere near what the American people think they are or what these levels should be. In addition, the Third World AIDS crisis continues to be transformed from being a nonethical issue (at least for us) to a situation where it is now coming to be recognized as perhaps the greatest ethical challenge of our time.

Finally, there is the war against Iraq. In some ways the war represents a culmination of all that is wrong with the United States in the world: The flouting of international law and international consensus, the bullying of small states, and the manipulative deception of why war was fought in the first place.

Beyond that, the gruesome images from the Abu Ghraib prison show, in stunning clarity, the utter contempt that Americans can have for "others." No matter how hard the George W. Bush administration attempts to put a humanitarian spin on matters, the reason why the war is so wrong is that it was not based on our best values but on our worst. And the ultimate tragedy of the war will be if we do not come to recognize this.

American society is at a juncture both politically and militarily, but, more importantly, I think we are at a moral crossroad. This, then, raises a third question: Have the American people become more moral since September 11, or has our society become less ethical? This question is still being addressed, and it is hoped that this book will help us answer it.

INTRODUCTION

Ethics in (and out of) American Life

We would all like to think that we are ethical people. We would all like to think that we work for corporations or business enterprises that are guided, in no small part, by ethical concerns. And, certainly, we would all like to think that our national government generally acts in an ethical and moral manner—or as ethically and morally as the world allows it to act. Finally, we all think that the world would be a far, far better place than it is if only people (other people, that is) acted more ethically than they do.

Few, then, would deny the enormous importance of ethics, and fewer still, I suppose, would deny that we need more ethics in our lives. Yet, despite this apparent interest in ethics and ethical behavior, I will argue here that we go to great lengths to avoid dealing with ethical issues and that this tendency to flee from moral concerns is particularly pronounced in the United States.

Obviously, the last sentence needs some further explanation. For one thing, how can the most religious people in the world—at least in terms of such things as belief in God, attendance at religious ceremonies, being touched by the power of angels, and so forth—be accused of removing themselves from a wide range of moral issues? But ethics is not religion, despite a great deal of overlap between the two.[1] Religion is ultimately based on a God, and the rules and doctrines of a religion are the means of worshiping this God. Morality or ethics,[2] on the other hand, is a concern with what we consider "right" or "just" or "good" behavior. Thus, although American religious beliefs reflect the very same self-absorption that our ethical values do—how else do we explain that 63 percent of the American people believe they will end up in heaven while only 1 percent think they will go to hell?—it is important not to conflate these two.

The other kind of response I would anticipate to the assertion that the American people flee from most of the moral issues around them is the answer that this is simply untrue. Rather, it can be said that the American people engage in debates about ethical issues all the time (sometimes in front of a national television audience), whether they are the sexual trysts of their presidents and legislators, the morality of surrogate motherhood, mothers who sleep with their daughter's boyfriend, and so on. It is true that Americans *do* talk a lot about ethical issues. However, the ethical issues that we address are invariably the small and the relatively inconsequential—the "easy" cases. What we run from are ethical issues that are not easy, especially those that address such fundamental questions as our place in the world. Our national power and prestige have given us license to follow a very narrow, parochial, and, ultimately, self-serving standard of ethics. What this book is about is the part of ethics that Americans generally leave out—the "uneasy" cases.[3] However, before turning to that, we will take a brief glance at how American society has tended to address ethical issues.

THINK SMALL: ETHICS AS INDIVIDUAL BEHAVIOR

Ethics as a field of study is divided into microlevel ethics—issues that individuals face in their daily lives—and macrolevel ethics—ethical issues of a more global concern.[4] What interests me is the relationship between these two. Although there is no inherent conflict between them and the two should serve as natural complements, microlevel ethics has essentially crowded out macrolevel ethics, which is to say that ethics has come to be both confined and defined in terms of the day-to-day behavior of individuals in very particular (but invariably rare) circumstances—and almost nothing else.

Perhaps the prime example of this dominance of microlevel ethics is Randy Cohen's popular column, "The Ethicist," that is run each Sunday in the *New York Times Magazine* and syndicated in other newspapers across the country. The column is in the form of questions from readers and funny, but insightful, responses from Cohen. Typical is this exchange:

> When I began to assemble the cabinet I bought from a large self-service warehouse, I discovered it was missing a drawer pull. I returned to the store intending to ask for a replacement, but it was crowded, and I assumed the pull would take a long time to find, so I swiped one from the display. I figure a floor manager will simply notice the missing pull and replace it, no harm done. Will I burn in hell?
>   Kenny Beckman, Almeda, California

Cohen's reply:

> You'll be singed in purgatory. As I suspect you realize, you stretched the definition of "self-service" beyond its ethical limits. If replacing the drawer pull had been a nearly insuperable task akin to the labors of Hercules, you might have considered—and, I hope, rejected—such dubious methods. (Hercules himself, you will recall, devised a clever—but not illegal—way to clean the Augean stables.) But in fact you faced only assumptions, imaginary barriers that you used to justify petty theft. I have no doubt that it is more convenient to act dishonestly; that's one of crime's most appealing features. (That and the chance of being played in the movies by Robert DeNiro—though admittedly he makes very few films about drawer pulls.) But what you did was indeed dishonest, and you shouldn't have done it. I suppose the store is lucky you didn't need to replace any missing floorboards.[5]

The problem with the column—more than that, the problem with the way we have come to think of ethics itself—is that the issues that are raised week in and week out are little more than "what should I have done" when faced with situations involving broken parts and display models, money that is found on the street, dogs that take liberties in my yard, and so on. The point is that after some period, it becomes almost natural for the reader to equate ethics with nothing more than the problems that we as individuals may (or may not) face every day. Beyond that, however, because most people would not steal from a model display or because we would try to locate the owner of lost money or because we do not throw dog crap onto a dog owner's lawn (although we certainly would like to), it becomes almost natural to conclude that we are indeed ethical people. The point is that these things are merely a very small part of what constitutes ethics, although it is definitely easy to pretend otherwise.[6]

THINK ABOUT WHAT YOU ARE TOLD TO THINK ABOUT: TEACHING "ETHICS"

You suspect that the person managing the group's coffee fund is pocketing the money. The person keeps saying that others aren't putting any money in the collection box, but you see that they are. The coffee supplies are always scarce, whereas there used to be extra money in the fund for doughnuts and such. This has been going on for a long time now. What should be done?

A. Discuss other possible collection solutions; for example, collecting money once a month from coffee drinkers, rotating coffee fund management.
B. Report the theft to Security.
C. Ignore it. No one else wants to manage the coffee fund.
D. Discontinue the coffee service.

Welcome to the world of business ethics, a high-growth industry if ever there was one. The hypothetical situation posited here comes from the workbook "Questions of Integrity: The Boeing Ethics Challenge" that is published by the Office of Ethics & Business Conduct at the Boeing Corporation.[7] Altogether, the Boeing "Ethics Challenge" consists of fifty-four different scenarios involving myriad problems that might be encountered in the workplace, and they are used to heighten awareness and to teach ethics at Boeing. These include the male employee who calls women "babe"; the manager who hires a buddy; the employee who copies computer software; the employee who drinks at lunch; the practical joker; the worker who swears; the employee who charges her time improperly; and so forth. Each scenario then provides four different answers, and employees who participate in this training are to select the answer that they think is the most ethical course of conduct. Training leaders have an answer section that has points assigned to each answer and then a rationale for the point total that is given for that answer. For those who might be interested, in terms of the scenario just posited, the "most" ethical answer is A, and the "least" ethical answer is D.

    A. (10 points). It may be correct that not all people are paying each time a cup of coffee is taken. By changing the collection method, you eliminate the opportunity for theft.

    B. (5 points). It is best to resolve the problem within the organization. If you are unable to resolve the problem, contact Security, because stealing is a violation of company rules.

    C. (0 points). Ignoring the problem won't resolve the concern but will result in elimination of the coffee services when the money for supplies runs out.

    D. (-5 points). While this would eliminate the theft issue, it would not benefit the coffee fund participants to stop the coffee service.

There is no question that the Boeing Ethics Challenge is, in a way, raising moral issues and engaging in ethical discourse and instruction. After all, the objectives of the Boeing Ethics Challenge have been neatly listed as follows:

Encourage employees to raise ethical issues with their supervisor or others.

Teach employees to address the ethical dilemmas they face.

Heighten awareness of Boeing values and standards.

Involve employees in a discussion rather than have them listen passively.

Create an atmosphere where the employees can learn by making the wrong decisions during the exercise so that they can make the right decisions in life.

Show that ethics is part of the daily business life at Boeing.

However, the problem with the Boeing Ethics Challenge (and many other tools for teaching ethics as well) is what remains unchallenged and thereby ignored. Let me offer two such issues: The first issue involves money. The top management at Boeing makes many, many times what ordinary workers do. This situation, of course, is by no means unique to Boeing. In fact, the average CEO now makes more than one thousand times what the average worker is paid (compared with thirty-nine times in 1970),[8] and this does not include many of the other "perks" that many executives enjoy. The point is that the fairness of the compensation structure at Boeing is itself an ethical issue, and one that would undoubtedly be far more important to ordinary workers than, say, the issue of missing money from the coffee fund or the ethics of dress on "casual Fridays."

Obviously, Boeing does not want its workers talking about whether it is fair or moral or right that the CEO of the corporation makes so much more than they do. Quite simply, Boeing's ethics challenge is not aimed at the corporation itself. By eliminating the issue of pay from their list of ethical issues at the workplace, the corporation deprives employees of an important avenue for addressing what is undoubtedly the most significant ethical issue in the relationship between employer and workers.

Also missing from the Boeing Ethics Challenge is the matter of who purchases Boeing products. After its merger with McDonnell-Douglas, Boeing became one of the largest civilian and military aerospace corporations in the world. One ethical topic that might engender all sorts of discussion is whether Boeing should sell military hardware to countries that might use these weapons to harm civilian populations or otherwise carry out human rights abuses.

One reason why there is so much resentment in the Arab world against the United States is that the United States is Israel's chief arms supplier. Included in the weapons that are sold to Israel are Boeing-manufactured Apache helicopters, and these helicopters have been used to carry out raids that have resulted in the deaths of civilians. To me, and perhaps to the workers at Boeing as well, where Boeing sells its military wares is at least as important as the issue of what to do with the employee who refers to women as "babes." However, one would never know this from the Boeing Ethics Challenge.

But perhaps the employees of Boeing do not rail against these exclusions. Take the issue of pay. It is not as if workers are not interested in how much money they are making. In fact, I think it is fair to say that there is no issue that concerns them more than this one. However, like the rest of us in this country, perhaps, they also have been socialized into thinking that issues of distribution—who gets and owns how much—simply do *not* raise moral issues. Thus, you can point out that the richest 1 percent of the population in the United States owns as much wealth as the bottom 90 percent, and you know from the look in the eyes of the people whom you are talking to that they are saying to themselves: what, exactly, is your point?[9] You can mention the fact that half of the population in the world lives—or, more accurately, *tries* to live—on less than two dollars a day and, again, you get a polite, but blank, stare. Somehow, matters of who gets how much money are *not* thought of as ethical issues, while someone cheating in a meaningless card game is. So perhaps the workers at Boeing do not naturally view the salary structure in the corporation as raising an ethical issue. However, there is also no doubt that the company is not about to encourage its workers to think otherwise.

The same is true of the issue of arms sales. To what extent does this society consider this an ethical issue? Since the mid-1970s, the United States has had legislation on the books that bans the sale of military weapons to countries that engage in serious human rights abuses.[10] Yet, these various laws have done little to change American practice. Not only is the United States the largest arms merchant in the world (by far), but many (arguably most) of the countries that we sell *our* weapons to engage in serious violations of human rights.[11] Moreover, note that nearly three-quarters of the arms sales that are made to the Third World are from the United States.[12] Still, I have yet to see a great deal of public outcry against these practices or even a general recognition that this constitutes an ethical issue.[13] The dominant view seems to be that we should make as much money selling our weapons as we can, and this is rationalized on the grounds that if we do not do so, some other country will. In that way, arms sales are viewed as economic issues, not as moral issues. All the while, arms sales grow virtually unabated.[14]

In sum, while the Boeing Ethics Challenge takes up certain kinds of ethical issues, it ignores many others. The ethical issues that are addressed happen to promote the corporation's own interests. Meanwhile, ethical issues that might benefit workers (salary) or those that might call into question larger business practices (arms sales) are systematically ignored.

The same thing goes on in our larger society as well. Although the American people want to think of themselves as moral beings, we also want to avoid moral issues that are going to greatly upset the lives that we live. So American society tends to do exactly what Boeing does: we deal with the moral issues that we wish to deal with (those that are more manageable and tend to make us look moral) while at the same time we ignore those moral issues that we do not want to deal with, invariably because they make us look far less moral than we would like to think we are.[15]

CHANGE HOW YOU THINK: "ETHICS" OUTSIDE THE UNITED STATES

One of the hallmarks of ethics is consistency. No matter what school of ethics one subscribes to, there will be a premium placed on being consistent. Almost by definition, to act inconsistently is to act unethically. In that way, the derisive expression "Do as I say not as I do" has real meaning for all of us because it underscores that it is wrong to profess one thing and then to do something completely at odds with those supposed beliefs.

This book is about consistency. In particular, it is concerned with the way in which Americans have come to apply one set of ethical (and legal) standards at home but a completely different set of standards (arguably no standards at all) outside the United States. Two points need to be made: The first is that this dichotomy itself constitutes an ethical issue, although it is an ethical issue that we have chosen to ignore. The second point is that while we might be fooling ourselves, it is quite certain that we have not been fooling anyone else. Americans do not understand why so much of the rest of the world "hates" the United States. What I am suggesting is that the very first thing we should examine is the moral code that we allow ourselves to live by.

Part I consists of five chapters—the five uneasy pieces—detailing various aspects of American inconsistency and hypocrisy in the world. Chapter 1 examines the curious and highly selective way that U.S. law regulates the overseas activities of U.S.-based multinational corporations, providing a few examples of some of the gross abuses that American corporations have committed in other lands. The point is that we could easily eliminate these abuses, simply by exporting many of our domestic standards to the overseas operations of American corporations so that they no longer will be operating in a legal (and ethical) vacuum. The fact that we have not done so says a good deal about our system of law, but it says even more about the kind of ethical standards we have given ourselves (and our corporations) license to operate under.

In contrast, there has been very little hesitancy in applying U.S. criminal law extraterritorially as we will see in chapter 2. One commentator has gone so far as to claim that this country's three greatest exports are now rock music, blue jeans, and American criminal law.[16] The problem is that only one part of the law leaves the United States. That is, while the *enforcement* provisions of the law have readily been applied outside the country, the *protections* afforded by the law—constitutional protections in particular—have not traveled well, and in the case of noncitizens, they almost have not traveled at all. Of course, all of this has tremendous implications for the government's "war on terrorism," as evidenced by the George W. Bush administration's claim that al Qaeda suspects being held by U.S. security forces at the American military base in Guantanamo Bay, Cuba, are without any constitutional protection—or protection under international law, for that matter.

Undoubtedly, the sharpest divide between our domestic notions of law and justice and those that exist internationally takes place in the nebulous area that we call "foreign affairs." Yet as we will see in chapter 3, certain foreign policy–related issues (especially those that relate to human rights) have been fairly well regulated by U.S. law and by American ethical standards, while others have not been. What smacks of inconsistency is that while U.S. courts have been quite willing to examine some of the human consequences of other governments' policies, these same courts have not been willing to examine the human consequences of our own actions in the world.

One area of foreign affairs that *is* based on moral concerns is our policy of refugee protection, which is the focus of chapter 4. What I show in this chapter is that American refugee policy has not been anywhere near as ethical as we have allowed ourselves to believe it is—or, more importantly, as it could be. For one thing, we have come to define "refugee" in such a way that many (arguably a majority) of the most vulnerable people in the world are not eligible for (our) protection. Along with that, we have taken any number of measures to prevent individuals from being able to even enter into our system of refugee protection in the first place. When these measures have failed to keep out as many refugees as we would like, what we have done is to systematically question whether those arriving at our borders truly are refugees. And in addition, the war on terrorism apparently has provided us with yet another rationale for closing our nation's borders to refugees.

Chapter 5 examines a bad habit that many Americans seem to possess, which is to ignore any and all evidence to the contrary and to declare ourselves (and our country) ethical—although our society does not use this exact terminology. Polling data show that the U.S. public is wildly optimistic (as well as ignorant, which might be fueling this optimism) about themselves and their government. But what we really are misguided about is how ethical the United States has been in the world. I focus on three such beliefs in this chapter: the generosity of American foreign aid, our consciousness of U.S. environmental practices, and our image of the United States as the "shining city on the hill," despite alliances with an alphabet (literally) of corrupt and brutal governments.

A CODA OF HOPE?

In sum, part I argues that Americans have an awfully strange sense of what ethics is and what constitutes ethical behavior, and for people who believe so fervently in the "rule of law," we repeatedly have allowed our government to apply different legal standards depending on locale, citizenship, and national self-interest. Yet, there have been some indications of change, and this change is the focus of part II.

For one thing, American society has started to come to terms with some aspects of our country's past, especially the horrible treatment of people in other lands. Chapter 6 focuses on the apologies that the U.S. government (on behalf of the American people) has issued to "others." Although these attempts to apologize have not been without problems, the fact that such measures are an important step toward becoming a far more ethical people than we are at present.[17]

In addition to recognizing our own inhumanity, the American people also have started to better recognize the humanity in other people. Chapter 7 focuses on various aspects of this change. The first is the transformation that has been (and is presently) taking place with respect to AIDS medicine in the Third World. Until a short time ago, the Third World AIDS plague was simply not considered an ethical issue as such—at least not for Western people. Rather, we distracted ourselves with other matters including the ethics of certain drug-testing practices. As we have done so often, we addressed ethics on our terms—but not on the terms of the millions of people throughout the world dying from this disease. This, however, has changed, and it has changed virtually overnight. What is perhaps even more remarkable is that Western governments (led by the United States) have started to back up some of their moral exhortations with concrete actions.

Another example of this ethical metamorphosis is the way in which the principle of humanitarian intervention has been rescued from desuetude. Or to place matters in historical perspective, there were more examples of humanitarian intervention in the previous decade than in the entirety of human history. There are at least some indications that our ethical standards are beginning to encompass issues of economic justice as well. Toward that end, the Jubilee 2000 movement helped to bring at least some measure of debt relief to a sizable number of desperately poor states and people. Beyond this, there even have been indications that Western countries and Western people are now starting to acknowledge what the rest of the world has long known: "globalization" has not been the godsend that it has been held out as being. And what has made this understanding possible is that distribution issues are no longer viewed solely as economic issues but, rather, as ethical issues as well.

POST–SEPTEMBER 11: WHICH ETHICS?

This book was started before September 11, 2001, and there is little question that its thesis will be severely tested by this great tragedy and all the events that have ensued from it. The overriding question addressed in the concluding chapter is whether the American people are more moral than they were before September 11—or have we become less moral?

On the one hand, the attack on the World Trade Center and the Pentagon could easily hurtle us back to our old ethics, which is to say the kind of ethics discussed in part I. As before, virtually all that would matter to us is American interests and American suffering, although we certainly would carry ourselves (and most certainly think of ourselves) as "compassionate" and "caring" and "moral" people.

We could, however, pursue a much different direction. What could happen—what morality dictates *should* happen—is that these attacks will actually assist in furthering the ethical transformation that was beginning to take place before September 11, 2001. For one thing, our own deep suffering should now help "us" to better understand the suffering of others. Certainly, the compassion and care for others displayed on September 11 represented American society at its best. The real question is whether these qualities will become the central core of a new American Ethics.

THE BOOK'S APPROACH

The final point is to inform the reader about my approach. The first thing to note is that the book makes every effort to be concrete and to avoid being abstract and overly theoretical. In that way, there is no discussion, let alone any application, of the various approaches of philosophy (utilitarianism, deontological theory, and virtue theory); there is no special effort to invoke any of the "great names" in political theory (i.e., Hobbes, Locke, Kant, and Rawls); and finally, there is no attempt to apply any of the theoretical traditions in international relations (realism, liberalism, and Marxism). In defending an approach similar to the one taken here, Jonathan Glover has written:

> It is possible to assume too readily that a set of moral principles simply needs to be "applied." The result can be the mechanical application of some form of utilitarianism, or list of precepts about justice, autonomy, benevolence and so on. When this happens, the direction of thought is all one way. The principles are taken for granted, or "derived" in a perfunctory way, and practical conclusions are deduced from them. What is missing is the sense of two-way interaction.[18]

Like Glover, my own feeling is that a "principles" approach too often obfuscates rather than illuminates. Thus, I am far more interested in testing the strength of a particular argument and much less interested in detailing what this or that principle might lead us to believe about the topic at hand.[19]

Related to this issue is the book's tone. Readers will quickly find out (if they have not done so already) that *Five Uneasy Pieces* is far more polemical than most other academic books. This is partly a matter of personal style, but it is also a matter of what is at issue here. In his "moral reckoning" against the Catholic Church,[20] Daniel Goldhagen attacks Western society's unwillingness to engage in what he calls "serious moral inquiry." Contrary to what he sees as the dominant thinking, Goldhagen argues that not only do we have the right to judge our institutions, but we have a duty to do so. What is necessary is that our judgments are based on fair and clear criteria that are transparent in their reasoning to conclusions. The charge of acting immorally is a very serious one, and certainly one that should not be made lightly. By the same token, however, when our institutions or our government act unethically, our condemnation of those practices should not be muted:

Because we cannot but judge, we might as well not be timid or furtive about doing it. Because judgments are rendered in any case, we ought to judge well. We ought to raise the task of judging to a central and valued practice, and carry it out regularly, in a sustained and concerted way.[21]

Make no mistake, this book also judges. However, what is being judged is not simply some part of our history or one of our institutions. Rather, we are being judged ourselves. The argument that I set forth in part I is that American society has some rather bizarre and warped ideas regarding ethics. Of course, this is not meant to suggest that everyone in this country shares these views—or anywhere even close to this. However, the evidence that I present is that in far too many cases our actions outside the United States are totally at odds with what we consider ethical behavior to consist of in the domestic realm. To me (and perhaps to others as well) these gross inconsistencies not only are unconscionable by themselves, but they cast strong doubt on our entire ethical system—and I do not shy away from saying so.

This leads to the issue of my level of analysis. For the most part, I am addressing myself to the ethics of American society and not the ethics of the U.S. government or the ethics of a particular presidential administration, although it is not always easy to separate where one begins and the other ends. We have a representative democracy in this country where government policies reflect (or at least are supposed to reflect) the wishes, the desires, the interests—and the ethics—of the broader population. In that way, I am not at all sympathetic to those who criticize the U.S. government but essentially praise the American people. We do not get off the hook that easily.

The last issue involves ethical standards. As already noted, I have made a concerted effort not to employ a principles approach. This, however, does not mean that I am not guided by any ethical standard. One that I especially like comes from a book project that I was a contributor to entitled *Ethics and International Affairs: Extent and Limits*. The editors of the volume, Jean-Marc Coicaud and Daniel Warner, set forth a standard of ethics that is based on creating and sustaining relationships:

Ethics is concerned with being as close to possible to realizing the idea, the positive idea, of what it is to be a human being. It is about approaching as closely as possible a sense of what is essentially *human* in our nature. In thinking and acting in an ethical manner, the individual makes himself a witness to what positively distinguishes humans: the quest for dignity. As such, ethics is a search for a reconciled presence—a reconciled presence to oneself, presence to others, presence to the world. This is also to say that ethics is not about the self in isolation. Ethics, fundamentally, has a social quality. It aims at integrating the existence and the fate of others into our vision of ourselves, into our thoughts and actions. It is about feeling that our individual lives extend to the lives of others. Ethics forces each of us to feel that our identity is also defined by our relations with others. It is the experience that, somehow, we owe something to others and that our ability to handle what we owe to others decides in some sense who we are.[22]

This book judges some of America's actions in the world. More than that, however, it is intended as an examination of our ethical standards themselves.

I

FIVE UNEASY PIECES

I

LAW, ETHiCS, AND THE OVERSEAS OPERATiONS OF U.S. MULTiNATiONAL CORPORATiONS

While fewer than 15 percent of the U.S. population own passports and less than this will ever travel to a foreign land, the exact opposite is true of U.S.-based multinational corporations, which enjoy an ever-increasing presence all over the globe. This chapter examines how badly some of our corporations have behaved in other lands and our government's response to these abuses.

We begin our analysis with the H.B. Fuller Company, a self-proclaimed "good citizen," based in St. Paul, Minnesota.[1] H.B. Fuller produces Resistol, a glue that thousands of Central American street children are addicted to. In 1992 the company's board of directors passed a resolution in favor of adding a noxious ingredient to its product, as its competitors had done, in order to discourage glue sniffing.[2] For undisclosed reasons, however, the corporation never did change its product, and Resistol continues to be the glue of choice for street children throughout Central America. In fact, there is even a name for these young addicts: "resistoleros."

Southern Peru Copper, an American corporation, operates a smelter plant in Ilo, Peru, that spews out some two thousand tons of sulfur dioxide a day into the air, or ten to fifteen times the limit for similar plants operating in the United States. Evoking images of the filth of London during the height of the Industrial Revolution, the *New York Times* provides this description of life in Ilo: " At times, the smoke from the smelter is so thick that it hovers over the city like a heavy fog, forcing motorists to turn on their headlights during the day and sending residents to hospitals and clinics coughing, wheezing, and vomiting. On those days, children are told to play indoors."[3] SPC is not violating any laws for the simple reason that Peru's very weak environmental laws have no emission standards.

Because of its toxicity and the fact that it causes sterility in men, the domestic (U.S.) application of the pesticide dibromochloropropane, better known as DBCP, has been illegal since 1977. Nonetheless, DBCP is still legally produced in the United States, and a number of American corporations—Dow Chemical, Occidental Petroleum, Del Monte Fruit, Chiquita Brands, and Dole Food among them—continue to use DBCP in their foreign operations. Because of these practices, tens of thousands of foreign workers in Third World countries have unknowingly been exposed to DBCP and have become sterile as a result.[4]

THE ETHICS OF OUR LAW . . .

Are these corporations engaging in unethical behavior? If thousands of teenagers in St. Paul, Minnesota, were zoned out on Resistol or if Southern Peru Copper were polluting Peru, Indiana, to the degree that it does Ilo, Peru, or if Dow Chemical were to apply DBCP within the United States, these corporations would be morally condemned. However, the point is that these "wrongs" are not taking place within the United States, and because they are not, there is a strong tendency to apply much different ethical standards—arguably no ethical standards at all—to the overseas practices of American corporations.[5]

One reason why our ethical standards seem to come to a screeching halt at our nation's borders is that our law does as well—or so we commonly think. Intuitively, the idea of applying U.S. law in a country like Peru seems as strange to us as the idea of applying Peruvian law in the United States. This certainly was the reaction of the U.S. Supreme Court the first time this issue was addressed. The case was *American Banana Co. v. United Fruit Co.*,[6] and the issue in the case was whether U.S. law (Sherman Antitrust Act) could be applied to monopolistic practices that took place outside the United States.[7] Writing the majority opinion for the Court, Justice Oliver Wendell Holmes found the entire premise of applying U.S. law outside the United States rather preposterous, and he expressed great surprise that the case was even before the Court:

> It is obvious that, however stated, the plaintiff's case depends on several rather startling propositions. In the first place, the acts causing the damage were done, so far as it appears, outside the jurisdiction of the United States and within that of other states. It is surprising to hear it argued that they were governed by the act of Congress.[8]

The reason, Holmes wrote, is that "the general and almost universal rule is that the character of any act as lawful or unlawful must be determined wholly by the law of the country where the act is done."[9]

Notwithstanding the Supreme Court's opinion in *American Banana*, within a short period U.S. law (or at least some of it) began to be given an extraterritorial reading by the American judiciary, especially the Supreme Court. As a result, U.S. monopoly laws—mind you, the same issue raised in *American Banana*—soon came to be applied outside the United States,[10] as were U.S. trademark law[11] and U.S. securities regulations.[12] In fact, a fair amount of domestic law has now come to be applied beyond the territorial boundaries of the United States, and one important reason for this is that this actually serves the interests of American corporations. In this way, for example, U.S. corporations not only are protected by trademark infringements that take place within the United States, but they are protected by those that are carried out beyond the country's borders as well.

The Supreme Court revisited this issue of the extraterritorial application of American law a few years ago in the case of *EEOC v. Arabian Am. Oil Co.*[13] The particular issue in this case was

whether a U.S. citizen working for an American corporation that
was doing business in Saudi Arabia was protected by the non-
discrimination provisions of the 1964 Civil Rights Act. The peti-
tioner, Ali Boureslan, originally from Lebanon, was a naturalized
U.S. citizen. The respondents were two Delaware corporations,
Arabian American Oil Co. (Aramco) and its subsidiary Aramco
Service Co. (ASC). Aramco's principal place of business is in
Dhahran, Saudi Arabia, and it is licensed to do business in
Houston, Texas. In 1979, ASC hired Boureslan as a cost engi-
neer in Houston. A year later he was transferred, at his request,
to work for Aramco in Saudi Arabia.

Boureslan remained with Aramco in Saudi Arabia until he
was discharged from the company in 1984. After filing a charge
of discrimination with the Equal Employment Opportunity Commission (EEOC), Boureslan initiated a lawsuit in federal court
seeking relief under Title VII of the Civil Rights Act of 1964 on
the grounds that he was harassed and ultimately discharged by
the corporation on account of his race, religion, and national origin.[14] Both the district court and the court of appeals dismissed
the suit on the basis that the Civil Rights Act does not apply
abroad. The U.S. Supreme Court upheld this decision.

In his majority opinion, Chief Justice Rehnquist wrote that
the Supreme Court assumes that Congress "legislates against
the backdrop of the presumption against extraterritoriality."[15]
However, the Court also reaffirmed what by now has become an
oft-repeated principle: "Congress has the authority to enforce its
laws beyond the territorial boundaries of the United States."[16]
Still, in order for American law to apply outside the country's
borders, there must be "the affirmative intention of Congress
clearly expressed."[17] The Court held that there was no such indication that Congress intended the Civil Rights Act to apply outside the United States, and Boureslan lost his case.[18]

Congress responded in 1991 by amending the Civil Rights Act
so that it now applies outside the United States.[19] As an aside,
one thing that should be noted about this legislation is that it
only protects employees who are working in the United States or
American citizens working for U.S.-based corporations overseas.[20] Thus, if Boureslan had remained a Lebanese citizen, Aramco could discriminate against him with impunity while he

was working for the company in Saudi Arabia—although it would not be able to do so if he was working in Houston. This, to me, is a strange kind of law and a strange kind of ethics. However, we will not pursue this issue.

Thus, contrary to what our intuitions might have told us originally, American law *has* been applied outside the United States— almost as a matter of course. Well, not exactly as a matter of course. What you would find if you went through the Supreme Court's jurisprudence is that the Court has sometimes taken very vague statutory language and (somehow) found the requisite Congressional intent that the law be applied extraterritorially, and at other times, it has taken statutory language that has been every bit as vague and (somehow) interpreted this language as not indicating the requisite Congressional intent.[21] But if you needed a rule of thumb it would be this: U.S. law that would serve to protect American corporations from foreign competition—monopoly law, trademark law, and securities law—*has* been interpreted by our judiciary as evincing a Congressional intent that the law be applied outside the United States. On the other hand, laws that might work to protect "foreign interests," especially the interests of foreign workers and citizens—U.S. environmental laws, health and safety laws, and labor laws— have been interpreted by our judiciary as *not* possessing an extraterritorial intent.

One could vigorously disagree with some of the Supreme Court decisions in this area. I certainly have done so.[22] In my view, Congress seldom has considered the extraterritorial application of legislation that it is considering. Because of this, the Supreme Court has essentially delegated to itself the ability to "make" law in this realm by interpreting some law as having an extraterritorial intent while denying such an intent to other, equally directionless, statutory language.[23]

In any event, the larger point is this: Congress has the power to enforce U.S. law outside the United States if it chooses to do so. This means that a company like Southern Peru Copper *could* be forced to follow U.S. environmental laws in its smelter plant in Ilo, Peru. United States law *could* mandate that H.B. Fuller Company add a noxious element so that none of the glue that it produces in the United States (including the glue that is sold for use in Central America) would be used for glue-sniffing purposes. And if Congress wanted to do so, it could easily write a law that not only would prohibit American corporations from using DBCP domestically, but it could prohibit American corporations from using this dangerous and harmful chemical in their foreign operations as well.

Note that in order to achieve these results, Congress would not have to create any kind of special legislation but only state its intention that U.S. environmental law or U.S. health and safety laws or both were to be applied extraterritorially.[24] In addition, the Congress could add a "foreign compulsion" provision (as it did in 1991 when it made the Civil Rights Act apply extraterritorially) that would state that U.S. law would be superseded if and when it came into conflict with the law of the host state. In other words, Southern Peru Copper would follow Peruvian law and not American law if there happened to be a conflict between the two. (As I have noted, now there is no conflict because Peru has virtually no environmental law.) The practical effect of applying U.S. law extraterritorially is that American corporations that are currently operating in certain countries without *any* regulation whatsoever would now be regulated in *some* manner—by the identical law and standards that regulate their domestic operations.[25]

The political willpower to regulate the overseas operations of American corporations in this manner is certainly not present, but neither is there a moral imperative to do so. The truth is that many Americans would view the issue of Nicaraguan teenagers sniffing Resistol glue as somehow different from our own teenagers sniffing it. Corporate behavior that places American children at risk is viewed as both a moral issue and a legal issue, whereas harm that our own corporations are causing children in other countries is, seemingly, not our concern.

There is only one[26] moral issue involving the overseas operations of U.S. multinational corporations that has been treated as such, and that is bribery. In 1977, Congress passed the Foreign Corrupt Practices Act,[27] which makes it unlawful for an American corporation to engage in bribery in another country—even if bribery is perfectly lawful in this other country. The reasoning behind this prohibition is that bribery is immoral. Not only is bribery immoral if it occurs within the United States, but Congress has decided that it is also immoral if an American corporation engages in bribery outside the United States. Somehow, in this particular case at least, our ethics do not change dramatically (or disappear altogether) once we go outside the country's borders. And since 1977, neither does our law.

Unfortunately, we have not followed the logic of the Foreign Corrupt Practices Act. Bribery is certainly immoral and the Foreign Corrupt Practices Act is to be applauded for taking an immoral act and making it illegal as well. The act stands for the proposition that American corporations are not allowed to engage in bribery even if the failure to do so will put them at a competitive disadvantage vis-à-vis companies in countries that do not prohibit bribery by their corporations. Unfortunately, what we have chosen to ignore is that bribery is no more immoral than what Southern Peru Copper is doing in Ilo, Peru, or what H.B. Fuller is doing in its Central American operations or what the likes of Dow Chemical and Del Monte and Dole are doing by using DBCP in Latin America. Yet, these immoral practices have not prompted a change in law in the same way that bribery has.[28]

In sum, Congress has had no problem mandating to American corporations that their overseas operations will be governed by U.S. monopoly law, by U.S. trademark law, by U.S. securities law, by U.S. tax law, by U.S. bribery law, by U.S. age discrimination law, and by U.S. civil rights law. However, Congress (and our judicial system) has shown absolutely no willingness to hold American corporations to U.S. environmental laws or U.S. health and safety laws or U.S. labor laws—even in situations where this inaction effectively means that American corporations are not governed by any law whatsoever and even in the face of overwhelming evidence that American corporations are causing severe harm to individuals in other lands.[29]

The rationale that is readily given is that applying U.S. law extraterritorially in this fashion would violate the sovereignty of the host state. What is indeed puzzling, however, is how we can legislate *some* aspects of the overseas operations of U.S.-based corporations when it serves our purposes and the purposes of our corporations to do so—and not see this as any kind of infringement on foreign sovereignty—but how we refuse to legislate *other* aspects of these operations when it would serve interests other than our own, most notably, the interests of foreign employees to work in a clean and safe environment and the interests of the general population of other countries to be free from massive levels of environmental harm brought about by American corporations.

. . . AND THE LAW BEHIND OUR "ETHICS"

Not only has American law been disappointing in very selectively regulating the behavior of U.S. corporations operating abroad, but the behavior of the American judiciary has been equally disappointing. And the reason I say this is that almost as a matter of course U.S. courts have dismissed lawsuits brought by foreigners who have alleged harm at the hands of American corporations.

Although myriad legal defenses have been proffered, the one most commonly relied on in summarily dismissing such suits goes by the Latin term *forum non conveniens*, which essentially means the forum is not a proper one. This doctrine gives courts the discretionary power to decline to hear a case when the convenience of the parties and the ends of justice will be better served if the action is brought and tried in another forum. In *Gulf Oil Corp. v. Gilbert*,[30] the Supreme Court first articulated the standards that federal courts should use in considering whether dismissal is appropriate based on the doctrine. After noting a number of factors, the Court held that "unless the balance is strongly in favor of the defendant, the plaintiff's choice of forum should rarely be disturbed."[31]

At first the law did not make any distinction between American and foreign plaintiffs, but that would change in *Piper Aircraft v. Reyno*[32] when the Supreme Court held that foreign plaintiffs are not to be accorded the same deference in the choice of forum as domestic plaintiffs. The results of this thinking have been nothing short of disastrous for foreign plaintiffs, and in case after case, foreign nationals who have had their cases dismissed in U.S. courts based on the doctrine of *forum non conveniens* have not been able to find justice anywhere else.[33] Perhaps this is simply a reflection of the lack of any merit to these claims. Or, in the alternative, perhaps this is a reflection of the fact that very few (if any) Third World countries have a legal system that is anywhere close to being able to deal with large-scale personal injury suits, and just as few have a system of law that could make corporations pay any substantial amount of money for the damages they have caused (e.g., the maximum judgment under Costa Rican law is $1,800).

One of the very few cases where foreign plaintiffs were able to make a personal injury claim in an American court for harm that occurred outside the United States is *Dow Chem. Co. v. Castro Alfaro*,[34] where the Texas Supreme Court allowed a personal injury suit filed by eighty-two Costa Rican banana workers against Dow Chemical and Shell Oil to proceed in Texas state courts. In a story that should sound familiar, for more than a decade Dow and Shell had manufactured and shipped DBCP to Castle & Cooke, the parent company of Standard Fruit, a Central American banana company. In the Texas litigation the trial court had granted the defendants' motion to dismiss on the basis of *forum non conveniens*. However, this result was overturned by the Court of Appeals in Texas and affirmed by a bitterly divided Texas Supreme Court. Judge Lloyd Doggett's concurring opinion (Texas Supreme Court) underscores the hypocrisy of the defendants' position, at the same time that it offers a different vision of both law and ethics:

> The banana plantation workers allegedly injured by DBCP were employed by an American company on American-owned land and grew Dole bananas for export solely to American tables. The chemical allegedly rendering the workers sterile was researched, formulated, tested, manufactured, labeled and shipped by an American company in the United States to another American company. The decision to manufacture DBCP for distribution and use in the third world was made by these two American companies in their corporate offices in the United States. Yet now Shell and Dow argue that the one part of this equation that should not be American is the legal consequences of their actions.[35]

Unfortunately, a case like *Castro Alfaro* remains the exception rather than the rule, although cracks have started to appear in the American legal edifice. Staying with the example of the banana pickers, since 1997 there have been two large settlements that have benefited thousands of agricultural workers, and a federal judge in New Orleans has opened the way for a lawsuit brought by three thousand Central Americans.[36] Meanwhile, a suit brought in federal district court in New York against ChevronTexaco for environmental damage done in Ecuador was dismissed on the basis of *forum non conveniens*, but on the condition that any final ruling and penalty imposed against the defendant corporation would be enforceable in the United States.[37] In addition, foreign governments also have started to respond. In 2000, Nicaragua passed a law for DBCP victims that required corporate defendants to put up a bond of $100,000 per case within three months of being served. This law, which the U.S. government aggressively opposed, has led to the filing of over four hundred cases seeking more than $9.6 billion in damages on behalf of seven thousand plaintiffs.[38]

Despite these advances, the larger point of this chapter is to show how inconsistent and self-serving the extraterritorial application of American law has been. The common fallacy is that American law does not apply outside the United States when in fact a great deal of U.S. law already is applied extraterritorially. The problem, at least from an ethical perspective, is how inconsistent and self-serving the extraterritorial application of U.S. law has been. United States law that serves to protect American interests has come to be applied outside the United States almost as a matter of course, while law that would serve to protect the interests of others has been kept at home.

In addition to this, the American judiciary has been extraordinarily hesitant to hold U.S.-based multinationals accountable for harms they have carried out in foreign lands even if this will result in the denial of any form of recovery for those harmed. Quite typical is the litigation brought against Southern Peru Copper, one of the corporations whose behavior we examined at the beginning of this chapter.[39] The Second Circuit Court of Appeals dismissed a suit brought by a group of Peruvian citizens on the grounds that causing high levels of environmental pollution within a state's borders is *not* a violation of international law, and thus is not actionable under the Alien Tort Statute (ATS) (which we will examine in some depth in chapter 3). If ethics is about extending our lives to the lives of others, it is easy to see just how unethical we have been.

2

CONFiNiNG OUR CONSTiTUTiON

While the previous chapter examined the inconsistent application of U.S. regulatory law overseas, there has been very little hesitancy in applying American criminal law extraterritorially.[1] However, the criminal law that is applied outside the United States is not the same law that is applied domestically. At home, the U.S. Constitution tempers the enforcement provisions of the law, whereas constitutional protections are virtually nonexistent in the international realm.[2] This dichotomy is not only bad law in terms of its inconsistency, but it is also very bad ethics in that it gives us license to treat "other" people in a manner in which we do not treat ourselves. Finally, this enforcement-protection dichotomy has some profound implications in a post–September 11 world, and we return to this issue at the close of the chapter.

A HYPOTHETICAL SCENARIO

To facilitate our discussion of these issues, consider the following hypothetical situation that we will return to throughout this chapter. José Rios operates a meatpacking plant in Bogota, Colombia. Rios is also a suspected drug kingpin. One morning, agents from the U.S. Drug Enforcement Agency (DEA) pay a visit to Rios's home where they attempt to interrogate him about drug-running activities. When Rios refuses to answer, the agents forcibly place him in restraints, and they begin to torture him. The torture goes on for two days before Rios signs the confession thrust in front of him stating that he is a drug trafficker. Ignoring the extradition treaty between Colombia and the United States, the DEA agents at this point take Rios on a government plane to the United States and place him in prison to await trial in this country.

In order to prepare their case against Rios, these same DEA agents return to his house in Bogota, and they begin to search the premises, albeit without a search warrant. The search produces incriminating evidence of drug trafficking that the government will seek to introduce at trial, along with Rios's confession.

Some time after this takes place, U.S. military personnel enter Rios's 14,000-acre plantation and meatpacking plant. At this time there is a civil war going on in Colombia, and United States military personnel are in that country to train Colombian troops. For whatever reasons, these American officials decide to confiscate Rios's plant and use it as a site for military training operations. What are Rios's rights concerning these actions by U.S. officials?

SEARCH AND SEIZURE

We begin our analysis with the search of Rios's premises. The leading case in this area is *United States v. Verdugo-Urquidez*,[3] which is based on a factual pattern that is quite similar to the situation at hand. Rene Martin Verdugo-Urquidez is a citizen and resident of Mexico who was believed to be one of the leaders of a large and violent drug-trafficking ring in Mexico. Based on a complaint charging the defendant with various narcotics-related offenses, DEA officials obtained a warrant for his arrest on August 3, 1985. In January 1986, Mexican authorities, after a discussion with U.S. officials, apprehended Verdugo-Urquidez in Mexico and transported him to the Border Patrol office in Calexico, California. There, U.S. Marshals placed him in custody and eventually moved him to a correctional center in San Diego.

After the arrest, DEA agents, working in tandem with Mexican officials, searched two of the accused's residences in Mexico.

During the search they found tally sheets, apparently computing the quantities of marijuana the defendant had smuggled into the United States. Verdugo-Urquidez sought to suppress this evidence at his criminal trial in the United States, contending that the search of his house without a search warrant constituted a violation of the Fourth Amendment of the Constitution, which reads:

> The right of the people to be secure in their persons, houses, papers and effects, against unreasonable searches and seizures, shall not be violated, and no Warrants shall issue but upon probable cause, supported by Oath or affirmation, and particularly describing the place to be searched, and the persons or things to be seized.

The district court agreed with Verdugo-Urquidez, and it granted his motion to suppress this evidence. A divided Ninth Circuit Court of Appeals affirmed this holding. However, the U.S. Supreme Court overturned this decision.

The premise of the Court's holding was that the Fourth Amendment was intended "to protect the people of the United States against arbitrary actions by their own Government; it was never suggested that the provision was intended to restrain the actions of the Federal Government against aliens outside of the United States territory."[4] Nevertheless, the Supreme Court also held that the use of the term "the people" in the amendment was intended to protect some individuals in addition to American citizens.

Who, then, are "the people"? Writing the Court's majority opinion, Chief Justice Rehnquist held that aliens with "substantial connections" to the United States are to be included in "the people" of the United States, and thus protected by the Fourth Amendment. Turning to the case before him, however, Rehnquist announced that Verdugo-Urquidez did not have the requisite connections to be considered one of the "governed," and thus the Fourth Amendment did not apply to him:

> When the search of his house in Mexico took place, he had been present in the United States for only a matter of days. We do not

think the applicability of the Fourth Amendment to the search of premises in Mexico should turn on the fortuitous circumstances of whether the custodian of its nonresident owner had or had not transported him to the United States at the time the search was made.[5]

One thing that weighed heavily in the Supreme Court's decision was the effect that an opposite holding might have on the conduct of U.S. foreign policy, which is a reflection of how far the "war on drugs" has gone in blurring many of the distinctions that had existed previously between the domestic and the international:

The United States frequently employs armed forces outside this country—over 200 times in our history—for the protection of American citizens or national security. Application of the Fourth Amendment to those circumstances could significantly disrupt the ability of the political branches to respond to foreign situations involving our national interest. Were [Verdugo-Urquidez] to prevail, aliens with no attachment to this country might well bring actions for damages to remedy claimed violations of the Fourth Amendment in foreign countries or in international waters.[6]

Near the end of the opinion, the Court once again alluded to the national security implications of applying the Fourth Amendment beyond the country's borders, positing a situation where troops would be employed to enforce our domestic law in other countries:

Some who violate our laws may live outside our borders under a regime quite different from that which obtains in this country. Situations threatening to important interests may arise half-way around the globe, situations which in the view of the political branches of our Government require an American response with armed force. If there are to be restrictions on searches and seizures which occur incident to such American action, they must be imposed by the political branches through diplomatic understanding, treaty or legislation.[7]

There are a number of problems with the Supreme Court's approach in *Verdugo-Urquidez*. For one thing there is the nebulousness of the "substantial connections" standard itself. The Supreme Court offered little guidance on when a foreign national would have the requisite connections in order to receive Fourth Amendment protection except to say that Verdugo-Urquidez's brief stint in the United States—in an American prison, no less— did not meet this standard. What, then, *would* a person have to do to meet this standard? Would owning property in the United States for some period of time qualify a person as having substantial connections? What about short but frequent trips to the United States—but what if these trips were to sell drugs or to commit some other criminal acts in this country? Or what if Rios had been a longtime informant for the U.S. government (as was the case of a much more famous drug dealer, former Panamanian strongman Manuel Noriega)—would these activities meet this standard?

Beyond this, if only those with substantial connections were to be afforded constitutional rights, then it would also stand to reason that searches of property owned by foreign nationals *within* the United States might not be governed by the Constitution if this constituted their only connection to the United States. This, of course, would go far in defeating the entire purpose of the Fourth Amendment. Finally, if one were to take the notion of substantial connections at face value, then there might be at least some American citizens who have virtually no connection to the United States. Perhaps these individuals have never lived in this country or ever visited the United States. Why are we so willing to grant constitutional rights to these individuals but deny these same rights to individuals who are being made subject to U.S. law?

Note the way in which Rehnquist uses the specter of war in order to deny basic constitutional rights in a situation that does not involve war at all but, rather, the enforcement of this country's criminal law—albeit in the context of the metaphorical war on drugs. Rehnquist is correct to acknowledge the blurred distinction between the domestic and the international in such settings. However, his means of dealing with this situation is not to imbue war or warlike settings with some form of constitutional protection, but to do just the opposite and remove such protection from a nonwar situation.

While the majority opinion was at least willing to grant constitutional protection to individuals other than American citizens, Justice Kennedy's concurring opinion would very much limit Fourth Amendment protection to the citizens of this country, at least with respect to searches conducted outside the territorial jurisdiction of the United States:

> In cases involving the extraterritorial application of the Constitution, we have taken care to state whether the person who is claiming its protection is a citizen, or an alien. The distinction between citizens and aliens follows from the undoubted proposition that the Constitution does not create, nor do general principles of law create, any juridical relation between our country and some undefined, limitless class of noncitizens who are beyond our territory.[8]

Kennedy should have stopped his analysis here because there is at least some intuitive logic in his distinction between citizens and noncitizens. However, Kennedy went further, and he tried to justify his opinion by pointing to all the logistical difficulties a warrant requirement would raise:

> If the search had occurred in a residence within the United States, I have little doubt that the full protections of the Fourth Amendment would apply. But that is not the case. The absence of local judges or magistrates available to issue warrants, the differing and perhaps unascertainable conceptions of reasonableness and privacy that prevail abroad, and the need to cooperate with foreign officials all indicate that the Fourth Amendment's warrant requirement should not apply in Mexico as it does in this country.[9]

I think that Kennedy is correct in his assertion that all searches conducted within the United States are (or at least should be) accorded Fourth Amendment protections. Such a rule is completely consonant with the reason why the Fourth Amendment exists in the first place: to protect against lawless activity on the part of the U.S. government. Yet, it is noteworthy that Kennedy merely assumes this fact without subjecting it to any form of analysis. And perhaps the reason he does so is that this does not readily fit into the citizen–noncitizen distinction that he is attempting to make.

With respect to all the logistical problems inherent in foreign searches that Kennedy makes reference to—where *do* you find magistrates in other countries who are conversant with American notions of due process, privacy, and the Fourth Amendment of the Constitution?—Kennedy is undoubtedly correct once again. After all, not many American judges would know anything about Mexican law (never mind the law of more distant states). Why, then, should we expect Mexican judges (or judges in any other country) to know very much about our law?

Fair enough. But then in the very next sentence Kennedy wipes away the logical edifice that he is attempting to erect by returning to his earlier point: "The rights of a citizen, as to whom the United States has continuing obligations, are not presented by this case."[10] In other words, *all* searches conducted by U.S. agents of property owned by U.S. citizens would be subjected to the Fourth Amendment. What this means in practice is that if American agents are searching the home of a U.S. citizen in, say, Thailand, these agents will either have to return to the United States to obtain a search warrant (not very likely) or have to get a search warrant from a judge in Thailand.[11] But what about all the problems that Kennedy has just mentioned in the sentences preceding this about the impossibility of locating magistrates in a foreign land who know anything about American law? Why is it that these concerns disappear when it is the home of a U.S. citizen that is being searched but play such an insurmountable role when we are speaking of a search involving a foreign national?

The better reasoned opinion is Justice Brennan's lengthy dissent, which is premised on the simple idea that U.S. constitutional principles should not be abandoned outside the United States when American law enforcement agents carry out operations extraterritorially. Brennan makes three arguments. The first is what he terms the "mutuality" that exists (or should exist) in the law. In Brennan's view, Verdugo-Urquidez had become part of the governed because of the government's actions that were being taken against him:

What the majority ignores . . . is the most obvious connection between Verdugo-Urquidez and the United States: he was investigated and is being prosecuted for violations of United States law and may well spend the rest of his life in a United States prison. The "sufficient connection" is supplied not by Verdugo-Urquidez, but by the Government. Respondent is entitled to the protections of the Fourth Amendment because our Government, by investigating him and attempting to hold him accountable under United States criminal laws, has treated him as a member of our community for purposes of enforcing our law. He has become, quite literally, one of the governed.[12]

Second, Brennan presents a much different conception of the Fourth Amendment than that given by the majority. In his view, the Fourth Amendment's focus is "on *what* the Government can and cannot do, and *how* it may act, not on *against whom* these actions may be taken."[13] In addition, Brennan repeatedly points to the great hypocrisy that would exist if the U.S. government could violate its own law in its operations in other countries, while at the same time lecturing the rest of the world on the need to follow the rule of law.

The final issue addressed in the Brennan dissent is the national security concerns raised in Rehnquist's majority opinion. Brennan begins by describing as "fanciful" the majority's depiction of U.S. armed forces being constrained by probable cause and search and seizure considerations. In his view there are any number of things that distinguish extraterritorial law enforcement from the conduct of American foreign policy. For one thing, "[m]any situations involving sensitive operations abroad likely would involve exigent circumstances such that the warrant requirement would be excused."[14] Second, situations in the latter category are more likely to be protected by sovereign immunity. And finally, almost as a catchall, Brennan argues that the Fourth Amendment will only apply in those (rare) instances where the government attempts to bring criminal action against a foreign national.

To sum up and to return to the hypothetical posed at the beginning of this chapter, if we say Rios is an American citizen, he will be accorded Fourth Amendment protection in any search of his home in Bogota, Colombia. However, he will not be afforded such protection if he is a foreign national unless he can prove that he has "substantial connections" with the United States—although it is not very clear what, exactly, gives rise to these connections.

One final point relates to when it is that constitutional violations take place. In his majority opinion, Rehnquist attempts to draw a distinction between the Fourth Amendment prohibition against unreasonable searches and seizures and the Fifth Amendment's protection against self-incrimination. In Rehnquist's view at least, "the people" language of the Fourth Amendment is different from the "no person" language found in the Fifth Amendment.[15] In his view the former is broader than the latter—although a very strong case could be made for just the opposite interpretation.

In any event, Rehnquist suggests that violations of these two amendments occur at different stages in the criminal procedure. In his view, Fifth Amendment violations only take place at trial, while Fourth Amendment violations occur at the time that the illegal search is carried out. He writes:

> The privilege against self-incrimination guaranteed by the Fifth Amendment is a fundamental trial right of criminal defendants. Although conduct by law enforcement officials prior to trial may ultimately impair that right, a constitutional violation occurs only at trial. The Fourth Amendment functions differently. It prohibits "unreasonable searches and seizures" whether or not the evidence is sought to be used in a criminal trial, and a violation of the Amendment is "fully accomplished" at the time of an unreasonable governmental intrusion. For purposes of this case, therefore, if there were a constitutional violation, it occurred solely in Mexico.[16]

What this position seems to suggest—perversely enough, in my view—is that somehow no violation of the law (or at least the Fifth Amendment) was committed at the time that Rios was tortured.[17] Instead, any such violation would arise at trial—but only if the confession was sought to be admitted into evidence. In any event, in the Rios scenario it would seem safe to say that the coerced confession would be excludable at his criminal trial.

At one point the Supreme Court held that "we have rejected the claim that aliens are entitled to Fifth Amendment rights outside the sovereign territory of the United States."[18] However, what would seem to distinguish the case cited by the Court, *Johnson v. Eisentrager*,[19] is that the aliens claiming Fifth Amendment rights in that case were enemy aliens of the United States who were outside the territorial jurisdiction of this country. This would not be the case with Rios who is merely facing criminal charges. On the other hand, as we will see in a moment, perhaps we should not be too hasty in imbuing noncitizens with any kind of constitutional protection.

A DIFFERENT KIND OF SEIZURE

Let us continue this analysis by examining the confiscation of Rios's meatpacking plant by U.S. military authorities. The leading case in this area is *Ramirez de Arellano v. Weinberger*, decided in 1984 by the Court of Appeals for the District of Columbia.[20] As you will see in a moment, there are a number of similarities to the present case. Temistocles Ramirez de Arellano is a U.S. citizen who owns and operates a meatpacking plant in Honduras, and Ramirez's claim is that the U.S. government had essentially confiscated his plant and put it to use as a military training site for Salvadoran soldiers.

Ramirez sued in U.S. federal court on behalf of himself and the six Honduran corporations that were wholly owned and controlled by him. The defendants, officers in the executive branch, denied these factual allegations and sought dismissal of the case. The district court agreed and dismissed the suit based on the political question doctrine (which we will see much more of in the next chapter). Surprisingly enough, however, the Court of Appeals overturned this dismissal. In the court's opinion, "the plaintiffs do not seek judicial monitoring of foreign policy in Central America, nor do they challenge United States relations with any foreign country. The case does not raise the specter of judicial control and management of United States foreign policy."[21] For one thing, the court pointed out that the case involved real property and not the allegation of any kind of personal injury:

"This is a paradigmatic issue for resolution by the Judiciary. The federal courts historically have resolved disputes over land, even when the United States military is occupying the property at issue."[22]

Running throughout the court's opinion was a deep sense of outrage—outrage that the U.S. government would dare treat an American citizen in this fashion. Typical is this kind of language: "The Executive's power to conduct foreign relations free from unwarranted supervision of the Judiciary cannot give the Executive *carte blanche* to trample the most fundamental liberty and property rights of this country's citizenry."[23] And this:

> The suggestion [by the defendants] that a United States citizen who is the sole beneficial owner of viable business operations does not have constitutional rights against United States government officials' threatened complete destruction of corporate assets is preposterous. If adopted by this court, the proposition would obliterate the constitutional property rights of many United States citizens abroad and would make a mockery of decades of United States policy on transnational investments.[24]

The Court of Appeals for the District of Columbia held in favor of Ramirez, and I believe that most people would agree that justice has indeed been served. The problem with this decision, at least from my perspective, is that that I am almost certain that there would have been a completely different result if Ramirez had been a Honduran citizen and not an American citizen. In other words, the case would have been readily dismissed if Ramirez had been a foreign national. The court purposely (and conveniently) avoided dealing with this issue in the context of the Honduran corporations this way:

> Because we hold that the United States plaintiffs have a protected property interest for the purposes of the claims asserted here and that they have standing to sue, we do not reach the question whether the alien Honduran corporations also have constitutional rights to judicial relief for the violations alleged here.
>
> We analyze this issue, as we must, based on the facts alleged by the plaintiffs. According to the plaintiffs' complaint, the operation is the enterprise of one man—a United States citizen.[25]

Why should citizenship matter so much? Of course, it could be rationalized (as the Supreme Court did in *Verdugo-Urquidez*) that the reason that U.S. citizens are protected is that there is a "juridical relation" between the U.S. government and U.S. citizens, while there is no such relationship between the U.S. government and noncitizens. However, on closer analysis what this juridical relation begins to sound like is little more than this: the United States can act pretty much any way that it wants in the world and get away with it—except when it involves the interests of American citizens.

In order to understand the depths of this differential treatment consider two recent and highly visible cases: The first involves Jennifer Harbury, a U.S. citizen who was married to Efrain Bamaca-Velasquez, a member of the Guatemalan National Revolutionary Union, a rebel organization that had fought against the various Guatemalan military dictatorships during the brutal war in that country. On March 12, 1992, Bamaca disappeared, and Harbury began a lonely public odyssey to locate him. Constantly blocking her were obstacles put in place by the Guatemalan and U.S. governments. In fact, American officials had informed Harbury that Bamaca was dead—at a time when he was still being held in captivity in Guatemala.

Harbury filed a lawsuit against the U.S. government essentially claiming two things: The first is that the U.S. government had played a direct role in Bamaca's torture and eventual death. The second is that by actively misleading her about Bamaca's fate, the U.S. government had interfered with her "access to courts." Strangely enough, the part of the lawsuit claiming that American agents had tortured and killed Bamaca was dismissed rather summarily, the court (citing *Verdugo-Urquidez*) holding that all these events had taken place outside the United States where aliens have few, if any, constitutional rights.[26]

Thus, while Harbury was allowed to proceed with her access to courts claim, she was not able to sue for Bamaca's torture and summary execution despite the court's ready acknowledgment that the behavior of American officials "shocked the conscience" of the court. Since when has lying become worse than murder?[27] The larger point is that U.S. courts have allowed Harbury, an

American citizen, to proceed against the U.S. government. How many of the tens of thousands of Guatemalans who were made widows and widowers by the war would be able to proceed in this fashion?

The second case of differential treatment involves John Walker Lindh, the American-turned-Taliban fighter who was captured in a foxhole in Afghanistan. Unlike his Afghan and Saudi brothers, many of whom are still languishing in subhuman conditions in camps in Afghanistan and in Guantanamo Bay, Cuba, Lindh was immediately whisked "home" and was scheduled to be brought to trial where he would have received the full panoply of constitutional rights. However, Lindh ended up pleading guilty, and he received a twenty-year prison sentence. The point is that membership certainly has its privileges, namely, constitutional protection. Yet, as we will see in the conclusion, even this so-called juridical relationship is now being threatened by the government's war on terrorism.

A REAL SEIZURE

The final issue involves the kidnapping of Rios. Once more there is legal precedent in this area to contend with: *United States v. Alvarez-Machain*.[28] Humberto Alvarez-Machain is a citizen and resident of Mexico. He was indicted in the United States for participating in the kidnapping and murder of U.S. Drug Enforcement Special Agent Enrique Camarena-Salazar and a Mexican pilot working with Camarena, Alfredo Zavala-Avelar. The DEA contends that Alvarez-Machain, a medical doctor, participated in the murder by prolonging Camarena's life so that others could torture and interrogate him. On April 2, 1990, Alvarez-Machain was forcibly kidnapped from his medical office in Guadalajara, Mexico, and flown to El Paso, Texas, where he was arrested by DEA agents. Both the district court and the court of appeals held that DEA agents were responsible for Alvarez-Machain's abduction, although they were not personally involved in it.[29]

Alvarez-Machain moved to dismiss the criminal indictment against him on the grounds that his abduction constituted "outrageous" governmental conduct and that the court lacked jurisdiction to try him, because he had been abducted in violation of an extradition treaty between the United States and Mexico.[30] The district court rejected the outrageous conduct claim but held that it lacked jurisdiction to try the defendant because his abduction violated the U.S.–Mexico Extradition Treaty. The district court, in turn, discharged Alvarez-Machain and ordered that he be returned to Mexico.[31]

The Ninth Circuit Court of Appeals affirmed the dismissal of the indictment relying on its previous holding in *United States v. Verdugo-Urquidez*, where the court had held that although the treaty did not expressly prohibit such abductions, such actions were directly contrary to the whole reason why a treaty was signed in the first place.[32] However, this holding was reversed by the Supreme Court.

The thrust of the Supreme Court's decision—hard as it might be to fathom—is that there was no violation of the U.S.–Mexico Extradition Treaty because there were no provisions in the treaty that actually proscribed abduction. The dissent answered by stating, as the two lower courts had, that the entire purpose of the extradition treaty was to prevent either the United States or Mexico from taking the law into their own hands in this fashion. Moreover, the dissent also pointed out that there is nothing in the treaty that prohibits torture or the execution of an accused, yet few would countenance this kind of behavior (let us hope). Notwithstanding the force and logic of these arguments, the majority steadfastly maintained its position, and it held that the case was governed by its decision in *Ker v. Illinois*,[33] a case decided more than a century ago before our present-day notions of due process were incorporated into our law.

Frederick Ker had been tried and convicted in an Illinois court for larceny. During the trial Ker claimed that he was unlawfully before the court because he had been kidnapped while he was living in Peru. At the request of the governor of Illinois, the president of the United States had sent an agent to Peru with a request that Ker be handed over pursuant to an extradition treaty between those two countries. However, the agent never submitted these orders to the Peruvian government but instead forcibly abducted Ker and brought him to the United States.

The Supreme Court found no basis for Ker's challenge.

Instead, the Supreme Court held that states could decide whether jurisdiction was valid in cases of forcible abduction, noting that "[t]here are authorities of the highest respectability which hold that forcible abduction is no sufficient reason why the party should not answer when brought within the jurisdiction of the court."[34]

Courts have routinely followed *Ker*, and there is only one case that I am aware of where a court has refused to permit prosecution because of a forcible abduction and that was *United States v. Toscanino*.[35] But what also has to be noted about *Toscanino* is that before the defendant was brought to the United States he had been tortured incessantly for nearly three weeks. The circuit court dismissed charges against Toscanino on two grounds: The first is that the United States, by virtue of its adherence to the UN Charter and the Charter of the Organization of American States (the abduction had taken place at the Uruguayan–Brazilian border), had agreed not to infringe on the territorial jurisdiction of other states as it had done through the forcible abduction. Second, the court applied a Fourth Amendment–type analysis holding that "the government should be denied the right to exploit its own illegal conduct, and when an accused is kidnapped and forcibly brought within the jurisdiction, the court's acquisition of power over his person represents the fruits of the government's exploitation of its own misconduct."[36]

Notwithstanding the brave and novel ruling in *Toscanino*, it is depressingly noteworthy that the Second Circuit Court of Appeals almost immediately limited its opinion in that case through its holding in *United States ex rel. Lujan v. Gengler*, where the court held that in order to divest itself of jurisdiction, the conduct of U.S. agents must be "of the most outrageous and reprehensible kind," resulting in the denial of due process.[37] Whether torturing Rios for two days, as posited in the hypothetical, would constitute this level of behavior is difficult to say. But think of what we are asking our judiciary to do: to distinguish between varying degrees of "outrageous behavior" in deciding whether to exercise jurisdiction over a defendant.

In sum, U.S. law allows American agents to carry out forcible abductions in other states, and for once citizenship does not carry any special privileges. That is, American citizens and noncitizens alike can be subjected to (some) torture and kidnapping, and yet according to the Supreme Court there is nothing in the Constitution or under international law that prohibits such practices. However, it also has to be said that it seems far more likely that foreigners will come to be treated in this manner than U.S. citizens will be, and for this reason the cruelty to be found in cases such as *Ker* and *Alvarez-Machain* will, in all likelihood, remain.

Let us return to the hypothetical that we started with one last time and ask a question that we have only glossed over: could it be that Rios is an innocent man? Once again, there is precedent in this area. After the Supreme Court had ruled against Alvarez-Machain, the case was returned to the district court for trial. However, there was no trial, because the presiding judge ruled that the charges against Alvarez-Machain were based on the "wildest speculation" and ordered him released.[38] Furthermore, the judge chastised federal prosecutors for failing to disclose that they had been told by Mexican officials prior to trial that Alvarez-Machain had nothing to do with the torture and death of Agent Camarena.[39] In a subsequent civil suit, the Ninth Circuit Court of Appeals allowed Alvarez-Machain's claim against the United States to proceed to trial.[40]

CIVIL LIBERTIES AND THE WAR ON TERRORISM

What we have seen in this chapter is that there is an enormous chasm between the enforcement of U.S. law outside the United States and the protections afforded by the Constitution. With the exception of those rare instances where an American citizen is involved, the Constitution has been confined in large part to the territorial borders of the United States, while at the same time the U.S. government has steadily increased the extraterritorial application and enforcement of American criminal law.

This enforcement–protection dichotomy has served as the basis for the government's decision to create Camp X-Ray in Guantanamo Bay, Cuba, where hundreds of suspected al Qaeda operatives are presently being held. Even though the detention is on a U.S. military base and under the sole direction and control of American military and security officials, the rationale for denying detainees *any* rights under the Constitution is that Camp X-Ray is outside the territorial jurisdiction of the United States. The sad thing is that the Supreme Court's territorial reading of the Constitution would seem to allow for this result; and the frightening thing is that there does not seem to be any kind of limiting principle.[41] Furthermore, the George W. Bush administration has gone so far as to say that the government reserves the "right" to detain suspected terrorists indefinitely, even those who have been acquitted of all charges by a military tribunal.

But if the Constitution does not apply in Cuba (or anywhere else outside the United States), what is to prevent the American government from doing this—or worse? As of this writing thirty-seven individuals who were in the custody of American officials in Afghanistan and Iraq have been killed—murdered might be a more accurate term. Moreover, it has become common for the United States to have its "dirty work" done by others, as suspects are routinely shipped to U.S. allies such as Saudi Arabia, Morocco, and Egypt, countries whose brutal torture methods have been widely documented in the State Department's own annual reports.[42]

Yet, the erosion of constitutional protection threatens to go even further. You will recall that one of the concerns expressed by Rehnquist in *Verdugo-Urquidez* was the prospect of having to apply constitutional protection to U.S. military actions overseas. What the war on terrorism is doing instead is bringing the war "home" by eliminating constitutional protections *within the United States* itself. One of the most (in)visible manifestations of this has been the secret detention of between fifteen hundred and two thousand men of Middle Eastern heritage. Another has been the very quick passage of what is commonly referred to as the USA Patriot Act,[43] which, among other things, allows the government to conduct "secret searches" whenever the major objective of the search is to collect evidence of terrorist activities, and to detain any alien for seven days if there are "reasonable grounds" to suspect he or she may be a terrorist or someone who is aiding terrorism. Furthermore, if the alien is charged with *any* crime (even if unrelated to terrorism), detention may continue for renewable six-month periods for as long as the person is deemed a "threat" to the national security of the United States. Beyond this, the Justice Department has announced that it plans to listen in on conversations between detainees and their attorneys whenever there is "reasonable suspicion" that these communications can pass on information or instructions to "further or facilitate" terrorism.

Another issue relates to the manner in which those accused of being terrorists will be tried. On November 13, 2001, Bush declared that any non-U.S. citizen suspected of terrorism might be tried in a military tribunal rather than in federal or state court (and this order would apply not only to soldiers captured in Afghanistan or individuals who have been arrested in other countries but to individuals who had been living in the United States as well). Responding to public outcry, the final set of rules announced on March 20, 2002, reduced some of the more controversial aspects of the original and draft proposals. For example, gone is the provision permitting a non-unanimous verdict for the death penalty, and the standard of proof for adjudication has been raised to the "reasonable doubt" standard. Still, these military tribunals would allow hearsay evidence as well as "secret evidence," thereby denying defendants the right to confront their accusers, and convictions would only require a two-thirds vote of the judges on these tribunals.

The final point relates to the manner in which the war on terrorism is even beginning to threaten the so-called juridical relationship between the U.S. government and American citizens. As we have seen in this chapter, U.S. citizens receive constitutional protection not only within the United States but beyond this country's borders as well. However, as the war on terrorism has expanded, and especially as several Americans have come to be categorized as "enemy combatants" (e.g., Yasser Esam Hamdi and José Padilla), the Constitution has shriveled to the point where it does not offer all that much protection to *anyone* accused of terrorist activities—and this now includes U.S. citizens.[44]

But perhaps another way of dealing with this problem is by severing the juridical relationship itself.[45] Toward that end, there is a proposed piece of legislation—the Domestic Security Enhancement Act (more commonly referred to as Patriot Act II)—that provides that any citizen (even native born) who supports even the lawful activities of an organization the executive branch deems terrorist is presumptively stripped of his or her American citizenship. In addition, the act would give the attorney general the authority to deport these (now) noncitizens if they are deemed a threat to our "national defense, foreign policy, or economic interests."

Where would these former U.S. citizens go? That seems to be their problem, because the act also allows the attorney general to deport people "to any country or region regardless of whether the country has a government." And if this fails, the act also allows the attorney general to detain indefinitely those who are ordered deported but cannot be removed because they are stateless. In sum, the war on terrorism already has done much to confine the protections of the Constitution—and perhaps this country's ethical values as well.

3

A CASE CALLED *KOOHi*

American Ethical and Legal Standards in the Realm of "Foreign Affairs"

If Congress adopted a foreign policy that resulted in the enslavement of our citizens or of other individuals, that policy might well be subject to challenge in domestic court under international law.

—Comm. of United States Citizens in Nicaragua v. Reagan, 859 F. 2d 929, 941 (D.C. Cir. 1988)

The result would be no different if the downing of the civilian plane had been deliberate rather than the result of error.

—Koohi v. United States, 976 F. 2d 1328, 1335 (9th Cir. 1992)

On July 3, 1988, a naval cruiser, the USS *Vincennes*, shot down a civilian Iranian Airbus, Iran Air flight 655, that had just taken off from the airport in Bandar Abbas, Iran, and was flying over the Persian Gulf. All 290 people abroad were killed. At the time of the incident, Iran was at war with Iraq, a country the United States would itself be fighting some three years later in what has come to be called the Persian Gulf War (and then again more than a decade later in the war against Iraq). The Iran–Iraq War was an especially brutal affair. One small aspect of this conflict was the so-called tanker war in which both Iran and Iraq targeted vessels carrying oil for the other side. In August 1986, Iran began to concentrate its attacks on ships calling at Kuwait ports, especially those flying the Kuwaiti flag. Kuwait appealed to the United States for help in protecting its shipping, and in March 1987 the United States announced that it would allow qualifying Kuwaiti tankers to reregister under the American flag, and that these ships would be protected by the United States Navy.

This, then, is how U.S. warships happened to be in the Persian Gulf region at that time. These ships would occasionally exchange fire with Iranian forces. Among the more widely publicized incidents were the following: On September 21, 1987, two U.S. naval helicopters fired on an Iranian landing craft, disabling the craft and killing some of the crew. On October 8, Iranian gunboats fired on a helicopter, and U.S. naval forces destroyed one of these gunboats. On October 16, naval forces destroyed an Iranian oil platform. On April 14, 1988, a U.S.-guided missile frigate struck a mine and was extensively damaged. In what appeared to be retaliatory action, U.S. ships proceeded to destroy three Iranian oil platforms and sank or damaged six Iranian naval vessels.

Earlier in the morning that Iran Air flight 655 was downed, antiaircraft guns fired on a reconnaissance helicopter sent to investigate reported activity by Iranian gunboats. The *Vincennes* then crossed into Iranian territorial waters and fired on Iranian gunboats. It was during this period that the civilian aircraft took flight. Apparently mistaking the plane for an Iranian F-14 fighter (although this has never been conceded by the Iranian government, which maintains to this day that the downing was purposeful), guns from the *Vincennes* opened fire.

Perhaps an American audience should not be surprised that a lawsuit (*Koohi v. United States*)[1] would follow in the wake of a great tragedy such as this, although there might be some discomfort at the prospect of our own judiciary becoming involved in matters that relate to foreign policy. Yet, as we will see in a moment, for the past quarter century federal courts in the United States have been very involved in international affairs of

048823

at least one sort, and that is by providing a forum for foreign citizens who have been harmed by their own government. In fact, it would be no exaggeration to say that U.S. courts have played a preeminent role in the advancement of international human rights.

What American courts have *not* been willing to do, however, is to provide any form of justice when foreign plaintiffs have alleged harm at the hands of the U.S. government. When such accusations have been made and complaints filed in federal court in this country, the American judicial system has taken refuge behind a battery of legal defenses. To give you some idea of just how deferential—supine even—the American judiciary has been, the court in *Koohi* not only dismissed the plaintiffs' suit (no surprise there, as you will see in a moment), but it went so far as to say that the result would have been exactly the same even if the downing of the plane had been *deliberate.* Ultimately what was unique about this case is that a diplomatic solution was eventually reached whereby the U.S. government agreed to pay $300,000 to each of the families of the wage-earning victims and $150,000 to each of the non-wage-earning victims—while, at the same time, admitting no fault.

But we are getting ahead of ourselves. We will return to *Koohi,* but before we do so, we will examine the manner in which American courts and U.S. law have (and have not) protected human rights. Much of what follows deals with law, but it also deals with ethics. For those things that do not directly affect the United States, we can act in a very ethical manner. In those cases we seek justice and we offer hope to those who have been victimized. However, we act in the exact opposite fashion whenever American interests are involved. In those cases we maintain the trappings of justice—lawsuits, procedural due process, judicial decisions, and so forth—but what we really give to those we have harmed is the illusion of justice and nothing more.

THE PROMISE OF *FILARTIGA*

The American judiciary has protected international human rights in a way that no other legal system in the world has even contemplated. The landmark case in this area is *Filartiga v. Pena-Irala*,[2] decided by the Second Circuit Court of Appeals in 1980. The decision was stunning for several reasons. One is that the case centered on the brutal practices of the Paraguayan military dictatorship, a subject of litigation that up to that point at least was certainly not very common in U.S. courts (or anywhere else for that matter). The second reason in many ways relates to the first: there was virtually no connection to the United States. Not only were all the people involved in the case Paraguayan nationals, but all (or nearly all) the relevant events took place in Paraguay as well. In fact, as we will see in a moment, the connection to the United States was fleeting at best. Still, the case was eventually heard in a federal court in this country and decided under American (as well as international) law. Not only was justice served in this particular case, but the decision set off a chain reaction, the ramifications of which continue to grow.

The facts of the case are as follows: Joelito Filartiga, the son of a prominent opponent of the ruling dictatorship in Paraguay, was tortured and killed by Paraguayan officials under the direction of Americo Norberto Pena-Irala, the chief of police of Asuncion, Paraguay. The Filartiga family's attempts to prosecute the agents responsible for the killing of their son proved to be futile, and at this point there was every indication that the Stroessner dictatorship would, once more, be able to carry out violence against its opponents with impunity.

After this, however, the deceased's sister, Dolly Filartiga, who at the time was living in the United States, learned that Pena-Irala, the police chief, was in New York on a visit. On behalf of her family, Filartiga filed a civil suit against Pena-Irala in federal district court in New York based on a federal statute passed by the very first Congress in 1789 (and essentially ignored thereafter). The law—the Alien Tort Statute—reads in its entirety: "The district courts shall have original jurisdiction of any civil action by an alien for a tort only, committed in violation of the law of nations or a treaty of the United States."[3]

As should be obvious, there really was no connection between the events that took place in Paraguay that served as a basis for the lawsuit and the United States. In fact, the *only* connection with the United States was that the torturer and murderer happened to be in the United States for some brief period. Why should this be enough to allow a suit to proceed in an American court and under American law? The district court apparently was of this view, and it dismissed the lawsuit. However, the Second Circuit Court of Appeals reversed this decision. In its ruling the court held the "law of nations" provided a "clear and unambiguous" prohibition against official torture. Furthermore, the court held that federal courts in the United States have jurisdiction to try cases against alleged torturers when "an alleged torturer is found and served with process by an alien within our borders."[4]

The case was then sent back to the district court, which in turn issued a $10 million default judgment in favor of the Filartigas because by this time Pena-Irala had left the United States and returned to Paraguay. To this day the Filartiga family has never collected a single dollar against this judgment. Yet, one would like to believe that they are convinced, as perhaps you may be, that at least some measure of justice has been achieved.

The *Filartiga* case essentially opened the floodgates for human rights litigation in the United States, and almost without exception foreign plaintiffs who have been victims of human rights abuses in other countries have been able to sue those who either directed or carried out these atrocities—so long as the defendant has been located in the United States and properly served.[5] Thus, several Argentine citizens were able to sue Argentine general Carlos Guillermo Suarez-Mason for human rights violations committed during that country's "Dirty War."[6] A group of Guatemalan plaintiffs were awarded a $47.5 million judgment against Guatemalan general Hector Gramajo for his role in the commission of massive levels of human rights abuses in that country.[7]

In *Abebe-Jiri v. Negewo*,[8] three women who were tortured in Ethiopia in the late 1970s successfully sued one of their torturers. In this case the judge awarded the plaintiffs $1.5 million for torture and other cruel, inhuman, or degrading treatment and for arbitrary detention. Six Haitians who had been detained and tortured because of their opposition to the regime won a default judgment against a former dictator;[9] another Haitian plaintiff who was mutilated by members of FRAPH, a paramilitary unit, has a default judgment pending.[10] In *Todd v. Panjaintan*,[11] a mother of a man killed in a massacre in East Timor successfully sued an Indonesian general living in Boston, while relatives of victims of the Rwandan genocide won a default judgment against the leader of a paramilitary group.[12]

In *Doe v. Karadzic* and *Kadic v. Karadzic*,[13] consolidated lawsuits were brought against the leader of the Bosnian-Serb forces alleging genocide, war crimes, crimes against humanity, rape and other torture, summary executions, and other abuses. The district court dismissed these cases, but the Second Circuit Court of Appeals reversed this decision.

The *Marcos*[14] litigation merits special attention. This case was the very first class action suit brought under the ATS, the first jury verdict (the other cases were default judgments), and, finally, the first case to be decided on the merits. The case consolidated five separate civil suits all alleging various forms of human rights abuses by former president (and dictator) Ferdinand Marcos. The district court had dismissed these suits based on what is called the Act of State doctrine, essentially, that the actions in question were official state policy (and thus not subject to review by the judiciary of another country). However, the Ninth Circuit Court of Appeals overturned this decision.

In sum, U.S. courts have played an extraordinarily important role in terms of the pursuit of international justice. Foreigners who otherwise would have had no means of recourse have been able to use our courts and our law to pursue those who were responsible for directing or carrying out abuses against them. Nearly two decades before the international effort to extradite and prosecute former Chilean dictator Augusto Pinochet, American courts had already established the principle that those who engage in human rights violations any place in the world can be called to account if they are found in the United States— although it should also be noted that the *Filartiga* principle has recently been challenged by the George W. Bush administration, and the issue is presently before the U.S. Supreme Court.[15] Still, as we will see in the next section, in many ways the *Filartiga* precedent (or at least its spirit) has been severely limited. And it not only has been limited by American law, but it has been limited by many of the same courts that have been so willing to hear cases involving human rights abuses committed by other governments—but, unfortunately, not by our own government.

LIMITATIONS ON OUR LAW—AND ON OUR ETHICS

Civil, but Not Criminal, Cases

As remarkable as ATS litigation has been, it is important to understand some of its limitations as well. For one thing, in order to be subjected to ATS litigation, those who direct or carry out human rights abuses must be located within the United States. A second limitation is the kind of legal proceeding that takes place. ATS suits are civil cases between private individuals and are not criminal actions, although it is not as if criminal charges are not available. In 1994 Congress amended the criminal code of the United States to provide that any U.S. national or any person physically located within the United States must be charged in a criminal action for torture committed against anyone anywhere in the world.[16] This criminal provision was part of the U.S. ratification of the Convention against Torture and Other Cruel, Inhuman or Degrading Treatment[17] (one of the few international conventions that the United States has signed, but that is a different matter).

Unfortunately and inexplicably, however, there has never been a single criminal action that has been brought under this law despite the presence of torturers within the United States (some of whom have been defendants in ATS suits)[18] and despite the explicit legal obligations that the U.S. government has willingly taken under the Torture Convention to "prosecute or extradite" any and all torturers within its territory.[19] In short, while the American system of justice has allowed foreign plaintiffs to bring civil lawsuits in our federal courts, the U.S. Department of Justice has not been willing to initiate a single criminal proceeding against those who have directed or carried out torture.

Individual, Not State, Behavior

Another limitation is that ATS lawsuits are only brought against individuals and not against the governments that employ these individuals. Thus, the suit in *Filartiga* was brought against a particular official of the Paraguayan government (Pena-Irala), but not against Paraguay itself, although as an agent of the state Pena-Irala was most assuredly carrying out the government's policy of silencing critics. The reason for this distinction is that states continue to enjoy sovereign immunity in much the same fashion that they did hundreds of years ago when it was thought that the king could do no wrong under the law. This view, however, is beginning to change, and one of the most notable changes has taken place under American law.

To best understand this, consider the case of Scott Nelson, a U.S. citizen who had been recruited to work in a state-run hospital in Saudi Arabia. Nelson accepted the position, moved to Saudi Arabia, and began his job. When he complained about certain practices at the hospital, Nelson was imprisoned and subjected to torture by Saudi security personnel. Nelson was eventually able to win his release (mainly through the efforts of a U.S. senator), and when he returned to the United States, he filed a lawsuit. If Nelson's torturers had somehow been found in the United States, he would have been able to sue them (as individuals) based on the Torture Victim Protection Act[20]—which is essentially the ATS for American citizens.

Presumably, those who tortured Nelson never traveled to the United States, but in any event, what Nelson did was to sue the Saudi Arabian government itself—the entity that had recruited him, the entity that had employed him, and, finally, the entity that the torturers worked for. The problem is that foreign states generally enjoy sovereign immunity in U.S. courts, subject to just a few exceptions.[21] The nearest possible exception that Nelson could come up with was that the Saudi government had engaged in "commercial activities" in the United States when it recruited him. However, the Supreme Court rejected this argument (as it should have), and it dismissed Nelson's suit against Saudi Arabia. In sum, an American citizen who has been imprisoned and tortured by a foreign government outside the United States was not able to sue that state—at least not in U.S. courts.[22]

Although Nelson lost, his case did attract some attention in Washington, D.C. Partly in response to this, in 1996 the U.S.

Congress passed the inelegantly titled Antiterrorism and Effective Death Penalty Act (AEDPA),[23] which, among other things, amended the Foreign Sovereign Immunity Act (FSIA)[24] to allow suits against foreign *states* for personal injury or death that was caused by an act of torture, for extrajudicial killing, for aircraft sabotage, for hostage taking, *or* for the provision of material support or resources for such an act if the act or provision of support is engaged in by an official agent of the foreign state.

All of this would seem to be for the good. For one thing, allowing suits against state officials but not against states was maintaining a distinction with very little difference behind it. After all, these officials are working for their government. Why, then, should you be able to sue one but not the other? The change would also seem to work toward better enforcement in the sense that Pena-Irala and every single other defendant who has been successfully sued in the United States for committing human rights abuses has been able to walk out of the courtroom and then out of the United States without having to pay a single cent. It is much more difficult for a "state" to disappear in this fashion. Finally, there is also the matter of resources. States have money for plaintiffs to pursue, while your run-of-the-mill torturer oftentimes does not, and already plaintiffs have been successful in suits brought against Cuba,[25] Iraq,[26] and Iran,[27] although the executive branch has thwarted most efforts at recovery.[28]

But what also has to be noted about the AEDPA is that the only countries that suit can be brought against are those that have been designated as terrorist states by the U.S. Department of State: Iraq, Iran, Libya, Cuba, North Korea, Syria, and Sudan. Ironically enough given its role in helping to change U.S. law, Saudi Arabia is not one of these states. Because of this, torture in Saudi Arabia would still not open the Saudi government to suit in the United States. There is, of course, little question that Saudi Arabia carries out terror—just ask Nelson. However, Saudi Arabia (and most other countries in the world, save a few) remains protected from suit.

There is a second important limitation in the AEDPA, and it is that the law only provides a cause of action for U.S. nationals, while nonnationals must pursue their claims against offending states in another forum, although it is not exactly clear where (or what) that forum might happen to be.[29] On one level it might only seem fair that American courts should give preference to claims that relate directly to the United States (although we will see the reversal of this idea in the following section). However, as we saw previously with respect to ATS litigation, the federal judiciary has thrown open its courtroom doors to *all* foreigners suing state officials who have brought harm to them (if and when these individuals can be found in the United States). In fact, at least for some time (until the Torture Victim Protection Act was passed), foreigners actually enjoyed *more* rights in the pursuit of human rights claims in American courts than U.S. citizens did. As an aside, think of how different (and better) the world would look if both aspects of American law were to be changed, that is, if *all* states that were engaged in human rights violations could be subjected to suit in U.S. court and not just the few that have been designated as terrorist states, and if *all* victims of human rights abuses could bring suit against these offending states and not just those who were U.S. citizens.[30]

A Much Different Set of Standards for American Activities . . .

The final limitation on our law, and perhaps an even greater limitation on our ethics, is that American courts have quickly run away from any allegations that the U.S. government itself might be responsible for violating the human rights of "others." That is to say that our supposedly independent judiciary—which has been so willing to entertain suits alleging human rights violations committed by foreign agents—has essentially shown no interest in protecting foreigners from the actions of American officials. Instead, U.S. courts almost appear to have taken on the role of promoting and protecting American national security interests—while at the same time ignoring the personal liberty interests of foreign citizens.

In *Sanchez-Espinoza v. Reagan*,[31] a group of twelve Nicaraguan civilians sued nine then-present or former officials of the executive branch (including President Ronald Reagan). The basis of the suit was that the U.S. government was providing military and financial support to the Contra rebel forces (who were trying to overthrow the Nicaraguan government), and that the Contras were, in turn, committing terror against civilian populations. A legal brief filed by the plaintiffs details some of this suffering:

> Twelve of the plaintiffs or their close family members have been subjected to murder, torture, mutilation, kidnapping and rape as a result of U.S.-sponsored paramilitary activities designed to ravage the civilian population in Nicaragua. The facts of the injuries to each of the plaintiffs or their family members reflect brutal, inhumane activities violative of fundamental laws of civilized nations. For example, plaintiff Maria Bustillo de Blandon, a resident of Nicaragua, saw her husband and five sons murdered and tortured by members of the Nicaraguan Democratic Front (FDN)— the main counterrevolutionary group funded by the federal defendants. On October 28, 1982, the contras entered her home, seized her husband, a lay pastor, and removed their five children from their beds. In front of the parents, the children were tied together, castrated, their ears cut off, and their throats slit. The father was then killed.[32]

The federal district court dismissed the plaintiffs' suit on the basis that the case raised a political issue rather than a legal one.[33] The Court of Appeals for the District of Columbia affirmed the dismissal but on the basis of the doctrine of sovereign immunity. What you will find in this case and those that follow is that the judiciary reasons that the U.S. government should be protected because what is being challenged is official government policy. What this ignores, of course, is that every single case discussed in the previous section—torture in Paraguay, rape in Bosnia, extrajudicial killings in Guatemala, massacres in East Timor, and so on—was also, in its own way, the policy (official or not) of each one of these states.

Returning to *Sanchez-Espinoza*, the Court of Appeals (in an opinion by then-judge Scalia) responded to the civilians' claim for monetary relief in this summary fashion:

> It would make a mockery of the doctrine of sovereign immunity if federal courts were authorized to sanction or enjoin, by judgments nominally against present or former Executive officers,

actions that are concededly and as a jurisdictional necessity, official actions of the United States. Such judgments would necessarily interfere with the public administration, or restrain the government from acting, or . . . compel it to act.[34]

Addressing (in a manner of speaking) the plaintiffs' claim for declaratory or injunctive relief, Scalia once more points to *how* policy is made, which then provides him with an excuse to ignore the *substance* of that policy, namely, that the U.S. government was arming, equipping, and training a group of murderous thugs:

> The support for military operations that we are asked to terminate has, if the allegations in the complaint are accepted as true, received the attention and approval of the President, the Secretary of State, the Secretary of Defense, and the Director of the CIA, and involves the conduct of our diplomatic relations with at least four sovereign states—Nicaragua, Costa Rica, Honduras, and Argentina. Whether or not this is, as the District Court thought, a matter so entirely committed to the care of the political branches as to preclude our considering the issue at all, we think it at least requires the withholding of discretionary relief.[35]

Despite the gross human rights abuses committed by the Contras, and notwithstanding the Contras' very close and intimate connection with the United States government, the court held that any relief in this matter would have to come from the political branches—the same branches of government that were accused of creating and implementing this policy in the first place—and not from the judicial branch.[36] The ultimate result of this approach, of course, is that neither the Congress nor the executive branch (and certainly not the judicial branch) has provided *any* form of compensation to the tens of thousands of civilians who were harmed or killed in this brutal civil war. The painful truth is that the litigation had absolutely no effect on the conduct of the war itself or its human toll.

The primary reason why human rights violations continue unabated in the world is the perverse (dis)incentive structure that exists: the state that carries out human rights abuses is also the same state that is supposed to police against them and to prosecute those responsible for carrying out violations. This, of course, is just not going to happen or at least will not happen very often. We can see this clearly when it relates to other states. What we have difficulty with is seeing it in ourselves. Yet, when the U.S. government is accused of carrying out human rights violations (beyond our territorial borders), the United States acts just as any other government does. That is not exactly true: our system of law does allow foreign nationals to file a suit against the U.S. government, and these cases usually do proceed to the "merits," at least providing the illusion that justice and the rule of law are in place. However, what is certain is that such cases will later be dismissed, invariably on the flimsiest and most irrelevant legal grounds imaginable. The result of this approach is that there seem to be no legal restrictions (and seemingly no ethical restrictions either) when the U.S. government operates outside the territorial boundaries of the United States.

Saltany v. Reagan[37] was a suit brought by a group of fifty-three Libyan plaintiffs (all civilians) who sued for personal and property damage caused by U.S. military air strikes in April 1986 in retaliation for the bombing of a disco in West Berlin that killed two U.S. servicemen. The defendants in the case included the president of the United States, various civilian and military officials of the U.S. government, and the U.S. government itself.

The district court dismissed the case in a summary fashion even though the court conceded that the alleged conduct by the defendants would have been "tortious" (i.e., actionable under law) if it were to be judged by any legal standards. However, the court did not apply such a standard—in fact, it did not apply *any* standard at all. Rather, the court dismissed the case on the grounds that the defendants had exercised "discretion in a myriad of contexts of utmost complexity and gravity, not to mention danger."[38] In addition, each of the defendants "acted, as duty required, in accordance with the orders of the commander-in-chief or a superior order."[39] Thus, on the basis that there was danger and complexity involved and that orders were being followed, the court held that the defendants were immune from suit.

One of the stranger features of the *Saltany* case is that despite some outward sympathy for the civilian plaintiffs' claims, the court also seemed deeply annoyed that such a suit was ever filed in the first place. At one point the court held:

> The plaintiffs, purportedly citizens or residents of Libya, cannot be presumed to be familiar with the rules of the United States. It is otherwise, however, with their counsel [former U.S. Attorney General Ramsey Clark]. The case offered no hope whatever of success, and plaintiffs' attorneys surely knew it.[40]

Continuing in this same vein:

> The injuries for which suit is brought is [sic] not insubstantial. It cannot, therefore, be said that the case is frivolous so much as it is audacious. The Court surmises it was brought as a public statement of protest of Presidential action with which counsel (and, to be sure, their clients) were in profound disagreement.[41]

In its haste to dismiss this "audacious" lawsuit, the court failed to realize any number of things. First, there was (and continues to be) a severe dispute regarding whether Libya was ever involved in the West Berlin bombing in the first place. That is to say, Libyan civilians were killed or harmed based on evidence that many (arguably most) of our allies have questioned. Second, even if Libyan agents were somehow involved, the retaliatory air raids violated the laws of war. Article 25 of the Hague Regulations of 1907 states: "The attack or bombardment, by whatever means, of towns, villages, dwellings, or buildings which are undefended, is prohibited." Finally, the court never provides any coherent reason why the lawsuit was unwarranted. Is the opinion to be read that there are no limits on U.S. activities in other countries? Or to phrase this another way: is there any number of foreign civilians who would have to be killed—particularly in a situation that did not involve "war"—before our judiciary would offer some measure of restitution, some measure of justice?

The American invasion of Panama in December 1989 resulted in the deaths of somewhere between several hundred and several thousand civilians. However, attempts to gain compensation on behalf of those who were harmed or killed have proven to be unsuccessful. In *McFarland v. Cheney*,[42] a suit was brought on behalf of a group of Panamanian civilians who suffered personal injury, property loss, and the death of loved ones during the American invasion. Many of the petitioners in the case had previously filed administrative service claims with the U.S. Army Claims Service seeking compensation for their losses and injuries, attempting to rely on a precedent used to compensate civilians harmed in the 1983 invasion of Grenada. However, the Army Claims Service rejected all the Panamanian compensation claims on the grounds that the various injuries had occurred during U.S. combat operations (which was true of the Grenada situation as well). The district court upheld this administrative finding, and this judgment was affirmed on appeal. While Panama has received some emergency assistance money from the United States, none of these funds have been set aside for the victims of the invasion.

. . . and with Very Little Assistance from International Law

My focus thus far has been on domestic law, and what should be clear is that U.S. law has offered virtually no protection to foreign nationals who have been harmed as the result of the conduct of American foreign policy. But note that international law has not done any better in this area. The reason for this is that international human rights law has concerned itself almost exclusively with the relationship between a state and the citizens of that same state. However, what has largely been ignored is the manner in which one state may aid and assist in the commission of human rights violations in another country.[43]

Throughout the 1980s the United States sought to overthrow the Sandinista regime in Nicaragua, and it pursued these policies mainly by arming and equipping a counterrevolutionary group that went by the name of the Contras. Notwithstanding Ronald Reagan's depiction of the Contras as the "moral equivalent of the founding fathers," they were a particularly brutal military force, and thousands of civilians in Nicaragua (including American citizens) were subjected to their armed attacks.

In response to this, Nicaragua brought a case against the United States before the International Court of Justice (ICJ).

Nicaragua claimed that the United States had violated international law in two different ways: The first was through actions that U.S. agents had carried out directly in Nicaragua—such as mining harbors. The second claim was that because of the very close relationship between the U.S. government and the Contra rebel forces, the U.S. government should bear at least some of the responsibility for the human rights violations carried out by the Contras.

In *Nicaragua v. United States*,[44] the ICJ held that the United States was in violation of customary international law for those actions in Nicaragua carried out directly by agents of the United States.[45] However, the court held that the United States was not responsible for any of the violations committed by the Contras, the reasoning being that there was no evidence that the U.S. government had exercised what essentially amounted to absolute control over the Contras' activities, holding that "in light of the evidence and material available to it, the Court is not satisfied that *all* the operations launched by the *contra* force, at *every* stage of the conflict, reflected strategy and tactics *wholly* devised by the United States."[46]

There are two problems with the *Nicaragua* decision. The first is that the level of "control" demanded by the court is virtually impossible to achieve.[47] The second problem is that the court treats "responsibility" in an either-or fashion. That is, under the ICJ's approach, a state that aids and assists an outlaw state is either fully responsible for the actions of the receiving state (if the state is somehow able to exercise this nearly impossible level of control) or not responsible at all. Thus, under the court's ruling, one state could arm and equip and be allied with a genocidal regime in another country—providing gas ovens to Nazi Germany or arming and equipping the Khmer Rouge in Cambodia or shipping machetes to the Hutus in Rwanda—and yet it would not bear *any* of the responsibility for the atrocities that followed unless it (somehow) exercised near-total control over the receiving state. Although what we are speaking about is the law on state responsibility, it does not take very much imagination to see that what we really are talking about is the law on state (non)-responsibility.

A much better rule of law (and certainly a far more ethical

result) would be to hold that when one state arms and equips another state with full knowledge that the receiving state engages in gross and systematic human rights violations and that it will use this military equipment to further these ends, the sending state will bear at least *some* of the responsibility for those human rights violations committed by the receiving state. Unfortunately, international law has not (yet) seemed to progress this far.[48] And because it has not, Western states can (and will) continue to sell their military hardware to even the cruelest and most brutal regimes, yet these same Western governments will not bear *any* of the consequences when tens of thousands are killed with these very same weapons—even if there was a very great likelihood of this occurring at the time the arms sales were being conducted. The problem is that state sovereignty and the law of state responsibility remain mired in the Dark Ages, and I would suggest that this is not coincidental given the way that it works to protect Western states. What needs to be asked is whether our ethical standards—which might assist us in prompting a change in the governing law—are not stuck in this same period as well.

RETURNING TO THE PERSIAN GULF

The downing of Iran Air flight 655 over the Persian Gulf gave rise to another lawsuit in addition to *Koohi*. In *Nejad v. United States*,[49] the plaintiffs were the families and economic dependents of four of the passengers. The defendants were the United States and twelve defense contractors who had supplied the ship with various types of military equipment. The district court dismissed the plaintiffs' case based on nothing more than the manner in which the navy operates:

> [I]t is indubitably clear that plaintiffs' claim calls into question the Navy's decision and actions in execution of those decisions. The conduct of such affairs are [*sic*] constitutionally committed to the President as Commander in Chief and to his military and naval subordinates.[50]

Koohi was based on the same set of facts and the disposition of the case was the same. What *is* surprising about *Koohi*, however, is not only the manner in which the court arrived at its holding but the harshness of its decision. Furthermore, what is so disturbing about the case are the legal and ethical implications that flow from the court's holding.

The district court readily dismissed the lawsuit on the basis that the case raised a nonjusticiable political question. Simply stated, this doctrine means that when a case raises a political issue rather than a legal one it should not be heard in a court of law. The Court of Appeals sharply disagreed with this reading of the law. Instead, the appellate court took note that "governmental operations are a traditional subject of damage actions in federal courts."[51] Taking this one step further, the court held that the lawsuit is not "rendered judicially unmanageable because the challenged conduct took place as part of an authorized military operation."[52] The Court of Appeals continued this line of reasoning by pointing out that the Supreme Court, in its decision in *The Paquete Habana* at the turn of the last century,[53] had made it clear that federal courts are capable of reviewing military decisions, particularly when those decisions are based on harm to civilians.

In addition, the Court of Appeals also made much of the fact that the plaintiffs were merely seeking monetary damages, rather than any kind of injunctive relief (such as asking the Court of Appeals to halt U.S. naval operations in the Persian Gulf), pointing out that "[d]amage actions are particularly judicially manageable."[54] Pursuing this theme further, the Court of Appeals held that because the plaintiffs were only seeking monetary damages, "the granting of relief will not draw the federal courts into conflict with the executive branch. Damage actions are particularly nonintrusive."[55]

Despite this promising start, however, the court then turned around almost immediately and dismissed the suit on the grounds that the U.S. government was immune from suit. According to the court, the governing law in this area is the Federal Tort Claims Act (FTCA),[56] which sets forth conditions under which a foreign plaintiff can sue the U.S. government.[57] Under the FTCA, the United States is liable for tort claims "in the same manner and to the same extent as a private individual under like circumstances." However, the act contains four exceptions to the waiver of sovereign immunity: the assault and battery exception, the combatant activities exception, the foreign country exception, and the discretionary function exception. It was the combatant activities exception that the appellate court relied on in dismissing the plaintiffs' claims.

Under this exception the U.S. government enjoys sovereign immunity concerning "[a]ny claim arising out of combatant activities of the military or naval forces, or the Coast Guard, during time of war."[58] The court in *Koohi* was of the opinion that the claims presented by the Iranian plaintiffs arose "during time of war."

The court acknowledged that the legislative history was silent with respect to the rationales behind the law, but the court posited three reasons for why the Congress might have created a wartimes exemption: The first is that while law is based on the idea that the prospect of liability is intended to make an actor more careful, in the court's view at least, due care was the *last* thing Congress was desirous of promoting.

> Congress certainly did not want our military personnel to exercise great caution at a time when bold and imaginative measures might be necessary to overcome enemy forces; nor did it want our soldiers, sailors, or airmen to be concerned about the possibility of tort liability when making life or death decisions in the midst of combat.[59]

The second rationale for the wartimes exemption suggested by the court was that law aims to secure justice and to provide a remedy for innocent victims of wrongful conduct. Once again, however, the court felt that these were *not* proper goals in a situation involving war. Instead, because war produces innumerable innocent victims on all sides of a conflict, it would "make little sense to single out for special compensation a few of these persons—usually enemy citizens—on the basis that they have suffered from the negligence of our military forces rather than from the overwhelming and pervasive violence which each side intentionally inflicts on the other."[60]

Finally, the court's third rationale, and perhaps its crudest and cruelest, is that law is intended to make people pay for doing wrong. However, what the court could not seem to fathom is why the U.S. government would purposely seek to punish itself if it did not have to do so. In other words, if you are in the position to make up the rules—and to stipulate who can or cannot sue you, at least in your own courts—you will make every attempt to work those rules to your own benefit. Thus, in the court's view, and apparently putting aside all notions of justice, it simply would not make sense for the United States to consent to be sued by citizens of countries we were at war with.

My sense is that most readers will agree with the court's ruling. Perhaps the rationales presented by the court are persuasive. Or perhaps it is the knowledge that a diplomatic solution of sorts was ultimately worked out by the governments of Iran and the United States, although I hasten to add that under such a scheme there are no assurances that any of the families of the deceased will actually receive any compensation. More likely, however, I believe that most will agree with the court's dismissal simply because we have become accustomed to separating how the United States acts and operates in the world and our own system of law from our own conception of justice and morality.

I disagree with the holding in *Koohi*, and I do so for a variety of reasons: First is the law itself. While there is a certain intuitive appeal to the idea that the law and the whole notion of legal compensation is anathema to a situation of massive violence and destruction—in other words, war—this rationale loses much of its force the further we get away from those kinds of situations. Admittedly, tensions were high in the Persian Gulf region and Iranian and American forces occasionally exchanged fire. In addition, a handful of soldiers had previously been killed and some property destroyed before the downing of the aircraft had taken place. This, however, is generally not what we think about when we think about warfare.[61]

But if we were to assume that the situation between the United States and Iran did in fact constitute war for purposes of sovereign immunity, then it is quite easy to think of a number of other situations—and a number of other countries—where the United States would similarly be at war. Consider the war on drugs in Latin America.[62] Would the activities of U.S. drug enforcement agents patrolling in helicopters in Bolivia in drug eradication activities meet the wartimes exemption? According to the holding in *Koohi*, I would see no reason why it would not. In that way, innocent bystanders caught up in the cross fire between DEA agents and members of drug cartels would have no avenue for redress—at least not against the United States.[63]

American peacekeeping operations in places like Bosnia, Kosovo, East Timor, and Haiti would also seem to fit under the wartimes exemption, which would mean that the U.S. government would be immune from responsibility for any and all actions (including atrocities) carried out by our military personnel in those countries. What is so hypocritical about this is that accountability only occurs when it serves the interests of the United States. The war in Afghanistan provides an excellent example of this hypocrisy. Hundreds if not thousands of Afghan civilians have been killed during the course of the fighting,[64] yet no member of the U.S. military nor the U.S. government itself has been called to account for its actions (the same is true of the war against Iraq as well). Interestingly enough, however, the American military was very quick to bring court martial charges when four Canadian soldiers were killed by "friendly fire" from U.S. forces,[65] although it should also be added that the United States Air Force later dropped manslaughter and assault charges.[66] The question is this: are the lives of Canadian soldiers somehow worth more than the lives of Afghan civilians or Iraqi civilians?

Beyond the problem of interpreting the word "war," there is perhaps a more serious problem, which is the court's determination that the wartimes exemption provision protects the U.S. government not only from *negligent* acts but also from actions against civilian populations that were *deliberate* and *purposeful*. As the court held unequivocally in *Koohi*:

> The result would be no different if the downing of the civilian plane had been deliberate rather than the result of error. The combatant activities exception applies whether U.S. military forces hit a prescribed or unintended target, whether those selecting the target act wisely or foolishly, whether the missiles we employ turn out to be "smart" or dumb, whether the target we choose performs the

function we believe it does or whether our choice of an object for destruction is a result of error or miscalculation. In other words, it simply does not matter for purposes of the "time of war" exemption whether the military makes or executes its decisions carefully or negligently, properly or improperly.[67]

In addition to being "bad law," the wartimes exemption also makes for bad politics. The U.S. government is founded on the principles of shared powers and a system of checks and balances. Yet, this is only true within our own domestic realm. In virtually anything even hinting of foreign affairs, judicial deference has become the ironclad rule.[68] The extreme (one hopes) is the language quoted at the beginning of the chapter from *Committee of United States Citizens Living in Nicaragua v. Reagan* where the Court of Appeals for the District of Columbia provided some rather scary insight into what it would take to *possibly* prompt some form of judicial review of the human consequences of U.S. foreign policy.

The case involved a suit by a group of American citizens living in Nicaragua who claimed to be targeted by the American-backed Contra rebels. Although the suit was dismissed, the court wanted to make assurances that judicial oversight was not always precluded, holding that "if Congress adopted a foreign policy that resulted in the enslavement of our citizens or of other individuals, that policy *might* well be subject to challenge in domestic court under international law."[69] Enslavement of our own citizens or the citizenry of another country—indeed!

On the positive side, I suppose, the appellate court in *Koohi* did not summarily dismiss the suit based on the political question doctrine as the district court had. Moreover, the court rejected out of hand nearly all the rationales that are commonly relied on by courts in removing themselves from issues involving "foreign affairs." Still, the court ultimately chose to treat the case as one involving a foreign affairs issue—war—as opposed to viewing this as a case involving the violation of personal and individual rights.

Finally, I also think that our law is unethical or at least easily lends itself to unethical results. One of the essential features of acting ethically is the removal of self-interest. This, in essence, is what John Rawls attempted to achieve in his widely known thought-experiment involving the Origin Position.[70] In a much less elegant (and ethical) way, this is what the court in *Koohi* touched on in its third rationale: given the opportunity, rule makers will invariably make rules that exonerate their own behavior. In the domestic sphere this is seldom possible. For one thing, those who make the rules also have to live with these same rules.

If lawmakers somehow do privilege themselves (or even attempt to do so), there is always the ballot box to remove such offenders from office. In addition, the U.S. Constitution holds lawmakers in check. For example, the Fourth Amendment protects all of us in this country—citizen and noncitizen alike—against unreasonable searches and seizures,[71] and when law enforcement agents violate the Constitution there will be severe consequences: evidence will be excluded at trial when the Fourth Amendment is violated, and in cases of particularly egregious law enforcement actions, the Supreme Court has created what have come to be known as *Bivens*-style remedies.[72]

Almost none of the checks that exist domestically exist in the international realm. Those who make the rules do not have to live with them, and foreigners who might object to the rules that have been created to govern *them* have no voice and no means of removing from office those who hand down these laws. This, of course, represents a much different conception of law and a much different conception of government. But it also represents a much different kind of ethics. Rather than removing self-interest, as ethical considerations invariably dictate in the domestic realm, what we actually seem to do in the international realm is to promote our own (national) self-interest instead. This is what our ethics seems to allow, and one reason for this is that this is what our law allows. The FTCA is a perfect example of this. Under this law *we* decide the circumstances under which *we* will allow foreigners to sue *us* in *our* courts for harm that *we* have brought on others. And of the universe of foreigners who have been harmed by the U.S. government only a subset—essentially citizens of friendly countries—have been granted an avenue of relief in American courts.[73]

To close this chapter, consider another small and long-forgotten incident. In 1993, former president George H. W. Bush undertook a trip to the Middle East where, among his other activities, he visited American troops who had fought in the 1991 Persian Gulf War. During the course of this trip, Kuwaiti authorities claimed to have uncovered a plan to assassinate Bush. Those who were behind the plot were arrested and taken into custody by Kuwaiti authorities.

Was justice carried out? Well it all depends on how you would define justice. Rather than allowing judicial proceedings to take their course—after all, perhaps there really *was* no assassination plot—President Bill Clinton initiated a military reprisal on Iraq.[74] As a result, Clinton's standing in popularity polls in this country increased by more than ten points overnight. Also as a result of our actions, but treated almost as an afterthought, more than twenty Iraqi civilians were killed in the bombing.[75]

Were our actions moral? The point is that morality is irrelevant, or at least it has been treated as such. We have been taught to believe that morality does not come into play when national security interests are at stake, and the American people have readily believed this. Therefore, the U.S. military could have killed 20 Iraqis, 200 Iraqis, 2,000 Iraqis, perhaps even 20,000 Iraqis in a retaliatory attack, and still we would not think of our actions as raising any kind of moral issue. What is also clear—is it not?—is that these actions would not be unlawful either. That is, if the families of any of the decedents had filed suit against the United States, the case would have met the fate of so many other suits alleging harm at the hands of the United States. The court would point out the same obvious (but essentially irrelevant) factors that previous courts have relied on in dismissing foreigners' claims: that there is a chain of command or that orders were being followed or that discretion was being exercised or that the president is the commander in chief of the armed forces or that we were at war with Iraq (even when we were not). In short, what is certain is that no U.S. court would address the issue of the deaths of these twenty Iraqi civilians.

How did we arrive at this end? For one thing, we have been conditioned to see foreign policy as being devoid of any legal or moral component. We also have been taught to believe that our actions do good in the world, and apparently we are willing to accept a large number of dead foreigners for this good. At the time of this writing, more than ten thousand Iraqi civilians have been killed in the ongoing war in that country. The point is that this has no point: Iraqi deaths are simply not a part of our ethical equation.

But perhaps this is the way that things have to be. Perhaps the expression "War is hell" speaks not only to the human suffering brought about by conflict but also to the anarchy and lawlessness engendered by fighting. But what this also means is that 290 Iranian citizens aboard a commercial airliner who are suddenly blown out of the sky have no legal recourse against the government that carried out this action. And according to the law—our own law—this would be true even if the downing of the aircraft had been deliberate rather than merely negligent. Still, the passengers and crew on Iran Air flight 655 (or at least their decedents) are privileged because a diplomatic solution was ultimately reached that resulted in the payment of some form of compensation. This is something that people all over the world—civilians, mind you, not soldiers—who have been harmed while the U.S. government has pursued its national security interests have been denied by American law, by American courts—and, ultimately, by the American people.

4

AMERiCAN REFUGEE POLiCY AND THE PRETENSE OF MORALiTY

Most ethical issues confront us directly. They stare us right in the face, and they demand that we deal with them—if we are able to. This, however, is not true for ethical issues that arise beyond our national borders. For the most part, we can literally tune out these issues when it serves our purposes to do so, and quite often, it serves our purposes to do so.[1] Consider the issue of world hunger. Currently approximately two billion of the six billion people who inhabit the earth do not have enough to eat, and tens of thousands of people die each day because of a lack of sustenance. Obviously, world hunger is (or at least should be) one of the great moral issues of our time. Yet, it is not a problem that those of us in Western states have to see or hear or think about if we do not want to. Instead, this problem exists a world apart from us—not only in terms of geography but in many respects from a moral perspective as well. Addressing himself to this very issue of how it is that world hunger is generally not considered to be an "ethical issue," Thomas Pogge has written about the consequences of this moral avoidance—for "us" as well as for "others":

> Moral norms, designed to protect the livelihood and dignity of the vulnerable, place burdens on the strong. If such norms are com-

pelling enough, the strong make an effort to comply. But they also, consciously or unconsciously, try to get around the norms by arranging their social world so as to minimize their burdens of compliance. Insofar as agents succeed in such norm avoidance, they can comply and still enjoy the advantages of their dominance. Such success, however, greatly reduces not merely the costs and opportunity costs of moral norms for the strong, but also the protection those norms afford the weak.[2]

Yet, there are times when ethical problems that we would otherwise ignore come knocking loudly at our door not only demanding our attention but demanding that we apply "our" moral standards to them. Such has been the case with refugees, individuals who flee their country of origin because they have a "well-founded fear" of persecution.

How have we responded to this ethical challenge? From our perspective we have responded very well. In the United States we can point to the fact that during the course of the past two decades we have admitted upward of two million refugees through an overseas quota refugee system and tens of thousands more have been granted refugee status after applying for asylum in this country. If anything, there is a decided feeling that perhaps the United States has done too much, as evidenced by the constant cries of "compassion fatigue." Could it really be that the U.S. government and the American people are *too* ethical?

The truth is something altogether different. At the present time upward of 90 percent of the world's refugees are being housed in Third World countries—very poor Third World countries, I might add—while only a relatively small percentage reside in Western states, and a smaller fraction of that resides in the United States. In addition, as I explain here, Western states (including the United States) have made virtually every effort to make these numbers that much smaller.

Our problem is not that we are too moral. No, the problem is that while we have been able to recognize the pressing moral claim that refugees present, we simply are not up to the task of meeting these demands—or anything even remotely approaching this. Western governments could simply acknowledge this and say that there are severe limits to what we can (or will) do in this realm and leave it at that. However, that would also mean that those of us living in the West would have to concede that we are far less ethical than we would like to think that we are. So what we have done is not to change our morals or our ethical framework but to change the moral problem itself.

What we have done is to worship at the altar of refugee protection like we always have, but we have taken any number of steps so that the ethical dilemma that refugees pose for us is considerably smaller and much easier for us to control. And if the truth were to be told, what we really would hope for is that this bothersome and burdensome ethical and political problem would simply disappear for us altogether. However, that is not going to happen (despite all the measures that we have taken toward that end), and in any event, refugees serve at least one useful purpose: they confirm for us that we are ethical people. Our problem (actually *their* problem) is that we have acted nowhere near as ethically in this realm as we think we have—or that we could have.

FRAMING THE ETHICAL DEBATE

Because refugee protection sits on the border between two moral spheres—"ours" and "theirs"—the manner in which the refugee issue is presented is particularly noteworthy.[3] Discussion of this issue invariably begins with the unquestioned assumption— announced as something rising to the level of a principle of international law—that nation-states enjoy absolute discretion in terms of entry.[4] This power to exclude entry on whatever terms a nation so chooses is viewed as an inherent sovereign right.[5] What this ignores is the manner in which this sovereign right has been (and continues to be) violated. It ignores the relatively short period of time that this principle has been established. Furthermore, it also ignores much of current state practice, particularly that of African countries that are marked by enormous migrations of human populations.

But perhaps the most fatal flaw in all of this is that this sovereign right is one that *we* enjoy, but it is not clear that others have enjoyed it as well. For one thing, it ignores the veritable invasion of European settlers into virtually every corner of the globe, from the fifteenth century to the last one. The British government is presently fearful of immigration from Commonwealth countries, the French of migration from francophone Africa, and so on. Funny how quickly we forget our own actions in the world. The effort here is not to drag up ancient history, because, in a number of ways, this is exactly what we are speaking about. But there is a marked tendency to go to the opposite extreme.

Beyond this, the notion of a sovereign right to control borders ignores the manner in which the sovereignty of other states (and it is always *other* states, and not ours) is repeatedly ignored today. Those of us living in Western states might wish to pretend that we are far removed from much of the mayhem in the Third World that has given rise to enormous levels of human migration and human suffering, but we are not. Instead, as a matter of course, Western countries have armed and equipped one war after another,[6] and they also have provided billions of dollars in foreign aid to the most corrupt and brutal dictatorships in the world.[7] The point is that the practices of "other" states are anything but the practices of other states. Instead, in varying degrees, they are *our* practices as well. However, it is very convenient for us to ignore all this.

This, then, is essentially how the issue of the ethics of refugee protection has come to be framed. After it is assumed that a state has absolute control over its borders, after it is assumed that countries like ours have absolutely no connection whatsoever with the creation of refugee flows in the first place, and, finally, after it is so readily and easily assumed that whatever absorptive capacity for refugees exists, Western states not only have reached that juncture but have actually gone far beyond it. At that point ethical issues involving refugee protection become relatively easy for us to deal with. This should be no surprise because we have set up the moral problem in exactly that fashion.

What we have done is to chop away most of the ethical issues that are (or should be) inherent in a discussion of refugee protection, leaving only a few relatively inconsequential issues for our ethical discourse. And after all this, we do in fact come across as fairly ethical beings. For example, most Western countries provide a plethora of administrative hearings for asylum seekers and, for the most part, these adhere to the highest standards of due process under our domestic law—although one should seriously question these outcomes because of their wild inconsistency.[8]

Living conditions for asylum seekers, particularly against the standards of the countries refugees are fleeing from, are quite good. In addition, Western governments do not return or deport all that many of those they have determined *not* to be refugees. Rather, Western states allow large numbers of nonrefugees (or, to be more accurate, those our governments have determined as such) to stay in our countries on some kind of humanitarian basis or simply through our own incompetent (but benevolent) way, because of our inability to deport many of those whose claims have been rejected. And finally, whenever our commitment to refugee protection is questioned, we can simply point to the number of refugees that we have admitted as proof positive of just how ethical we happen to be. This, in sum, is what we have attempted to pass off as a discussion of the ethics of refugee protection.

REDEFINING THE PROBLEM: THE PERVERSION OF THE REFUGEE DEFINITION

According to the United Nations Refugee Convention definition (which is essentially the definition under U.S. law as well) a refugee is an individual who,

> owing to well-founded fear of being persecuted for reasons of race, religion, nationality, membership of a social group or political opinion, is outside the country of his nationality and is unable or, owing to such fear, is unwilling to avail himself of the protection of that country; or who, not having a nationality and being outside the country of his former habitual residence . . . is unable or, owing to such fear, is unwilling to return to it.[9]

The purpose of refugee protection—this much should be obvious—is to protect defenseless people. However, this end has somehow become lost or perverted. For a variety of reasons, but mainly because of our own need to greatly reduce the size and scope of our ethical obligations, what we have done is to interpret the refugee definition in such a way that many (arguably most) of the most vulnerable people in the world are left unprotected—at least by us.[10]

The most significant perversion of the Refugee Convention definition is the ready acceptance of the idea that individuals who are merely fleeing war are (somehow) not refugees. Wars, of course, have always brought with them great harm and suffering. However, this problem has been greatly exacerbated as the nature of warfare has changed markedly, and in most conflicts now, civilian populations are the intended targets, which is why upward of 90 percent of the casualties in wars are civilians.

Consider by way of example the terrible civil wars in Central America in the 1980s and the U.S. (non)response in terms of refugee protection. Upward of four hundred thousand civilians were killed in wars in Nicaragua, El Salvador, and Guatemala. Yet, despite these incredible levels of human carnage, many refugee lawyers (especially those working for the U.S. government) took the position that a large majority of refugee claims from Central America were manifestly unfounded, and should be treated as such.[11] All that individuals fleeing from these afflicted countries could show is that they feared for their lives—a very real fear, as the empirical evidence shows quite clearly. This, however, was not good enough—or at least we deemed it not good enough for *us*—and because of this, the vast majority (on the order of 97 percent and higher) of refugee claims from El Salvador and Guatemala were rejected.[12] In some strange and perverse way, then, even though two hundred thousand civilians were killed in Guatemala and another seventy-five thousand in El Salvador, there were essentially no refugees from these countries.

A second perversion of the refugee definition, and another means by which we have sought to limit the moral problem that refugees pose for us, is found in the requirement that has been read into the law that an individual must show that he or she has been "singled out" for persecution. According to this view, large-scale suffering and gross and systematic levels of human rights abuses in another country are not enough to ensure that a particular individual applicant receives refugee protection. In fact, rather than *helping* this claimant, these things will actually work *against* the person's asylum application. The rationale (somehow) is that conditions are very bad in your country of origin, but they are bad for everybody. But because they are bad for everybody, unless the applicant can show that he or she is placed in some kind of special danger, a refusal of granting refugee status is not unwarranted. I have described this phenomenon elsewhere as the "perverse-inverse" relationship between levels of human rights abuses and the granting of refugee protection.[13] As the former goes up, the latter (inexplicably and immorally) goes down.

What is behind this policy, of course, is the fear of the slippery slope. That is, if our government were to grant refugee status to one person from one of the world's hellholes, we would, of logical necessity, have to provide it to many other people from that same country (assuming, of course, that all would have the means of arriving at our borders, which is a very large assumption). These are real fears that I do not mean to underestimate or denigrate. But quite often the result of this kind of thinking is that those who are in the most need of protection—especially individuals who live in countries where violence is of epidemic proportions—are the *least* likely to be recognized as refugees. And this goes directly contrary to the entire purpose for why we provide (or should provide) refugee protection in the first place.

Another way of substantially decreasing the number of those eligible for refugee protection is for the receiving country to demand that the persecution in question be carried out by the state. In theory such a requirement is justifiable enough. Private squabbles should not invoke refugee protection. However, purposely or not, this requirement misses a number of things. One is that it is not uncommon for state actors to pose as other than state actors. In addition, such a requirement also ignores that in a number of countries state officials readily allow private vigilante groups to commit large-scale human rights abuses. Finally, and most important of all, to innocent victims it matters little where the violence that is directed at them comes from. What matters most to them, of course, is the desperate need for protection.

The Refugee Convention definition also has been perverted by what we demand that refugees prove to us. In *INS v. Elias-Zacarias*,[14] the U.S. Supreme Court denied refugee status to a Guatemalan teenager (Elias-Zacarias) whom guerrilla soldiers threatened when he refused to join their group and who then fled to the United States. The Supreme Court held that Elias-Zacarias's refusal to join the guerrillas was not necessarily an expression of a political opinion, and that there were any number of nonpolitical reasons why Elias-Zacarias might not have wanted to join a guerrilla organization. Furthermore, the Court held that the mere desire not to take sides in a civil conflict does not constitute in and of itself a political opinion. Thus, even if Elias-Zacarias could prove persecution, he would not be able to show that this persecution was "on account of" his political opinion (or any of the other four enumerated criteria).

Beyond this, however, the Court held that even if remaining neutral could be considered to be a political opinion, a refugee claimant must also show that he or she has a well-founded fear that the guerrillas will persecute him on the basis of this opinion, rather than because of his refusal to fight with them or for some other reason. In other words, in order to be granted refugee status in the United States, an asylum claimant must offer some proof of why the persecutor is persecuting him. Perhaps conceding the near impossibility of this task, the Court held that a claimant did not need to provide "direct proof of his persecutor's intent."[15] However, the Court continued, "since the statute makes motive critical, he must provide *some* evidence of it, direct or circumstantial."[16] And if the refugee claimant is not able to prove this—would you kindly stop torturing me for a moment and sign an affidavit stating that you are persecuting me because you find my political opinions objectionable—the refugee can be returned to his or her country of origin, notwithstanding the grave danger (death even) the refugee may face on his or her return.

PREVENTING THE ETHICAL PROBLEM FROM ARISING IN THE FIRST PLACE

Despite the presentation thus far of what might seem rather damning evidence of state practice through which receiving states have defined who a refugee is with a decided eye toward protecting and promoting their own national interests, most governments do follow the legal demands of the *nonrefoulement* principle, which is to say that governments generally do not purposely send refugees back to their country of origin if there is a substantial likelihood that these individuals will be harmed or their freedom taken away.[17] What has happened instead, however, is that states have gone to incredible lengths to prevent individuals from getting into the refugee "system" in the first place.

In 1993 the Supreme Court handed down a disturbing 8–1 decision in the case of *Sale v. Haitians Ctr. Council, Inc.*[18] The question in this case was the legality of the U.S. government's Haitian interdiction program whereby Coast Guard cutters intercepted and returned all boats (rafts, really) from Haiti. At first, asylum hearings were provided. However, in due time this charade of charity and fairness was mercifully ended. Up until the Haitian coup of 1991, 22,716 Haitians had been stopped and interviewed on board U.S. Coast Guard cutters, but a grand total of 28 people had been allowed to proceed to the United States for further pursuit of their asylum claim.[19] Mind you, human rights conditions in Haiti have consistently ranked as being among the worst in this hemisphere.

The Supreme Court upheld the legality of the interdiction program, and it did so on the grounds that the *nonrefoulement* provisions in American (and international) law that dictate that a person cannot be returned to a country where his life or freedom would be threatened were only applicable *after* a person had reached the territorial jurisdiction of the United States.[20] The Court arrived at its decision after a tortuous analysis of what the word "return" meant, ultimately holding that a person could be returned only if he or she had arrived someplace else, which is also to say that the act of turning a person's boat around in midjourney (say on the high seas) and forcibly taking this person back to his or her country of origin does not constitute a return.

The case elicited an enormous amount of criticism, as well it should. One problem is that the decision fails the "certain death" test, and thus, it is contrary to why we have a system of refugee protection in the first place. Under the Court's holding, the U.S. government could forcibly and personally hand over an individual back to his or her persecutors—knowing full well that this person would be harmed or killed—yet there would be nothing illegal about this practice (under U.S. law or international law, or at least the Court's interpretation of them) so long as the person had never reached American soil, and in the case of Haitians at least, we have shown that we will do virtually everything in our power to make sure that they never reach the United States.

The *Sale* case is not only horrible law, but it is horrible ethics as well. To posit a situation where we would have one set of obligations to a person who has arrived at our shore but a completely different set of obligations (seemingly no obligations at all) to an individual swimming mightily but who is a few cruel feet from reaching our borders is simply to make a distinction without a difference. In addition, what possibly can be said in defense of a law that would allow an innocent victim to be sent back to his country of origin and certain death other than the fact that this law—which is (or at least was) intended to protect individuals—has completely strayed from its original meaning?

It is very easy to criticize the Court's decision in *Sale*. However, in many ways the policies of other Western countries are no less objectionable and no less inhumane than the practices of the U.S. government on the high seas, although certainly far less visible and dramatic.[21] The double-barrel policies I am talking about are the implementation of visa requirements against nationals of certain countries and, along with that, the enactment of carrier sanctions against airlines that have been found (after the fact) transporting passengers without valid passports and visas.

In a truly moral universe, there would be *no* visa requirements for nationals of countries experiencing gross and systematic levels of human rights abuses. The reason for this, quite simply, is that these are conditions under which some number of people will be in need of refugee protection in another country. This, however, is not the moral universe that we live in at present. In fact, receiving countries do just the opposite as a matter of course. That is, it is quite common for them to suddenly require visas for nationals of countries whenever human rights conditions become grave and there is even the slightest trickle of refugees fleeing from these lands. If the aim of the visa requirement was to try to ensure some kind of order to the outflow or perhaps offer some avenue for individuals to begin to apply for refugee status or both, one might be willing to accept such a policy. But order is not the aim. Rather the goal of these policies is to prevent individuals from even being able to make an application for refugee protection.

Another mechanism for severely reducing the number of asylum claims is through the adoption of what are called safe third-country policies. There are two aspects to this: The first is that countries will simply bar an asylum application if it is determined that an asylum seeker has traveled through "safe countries of asylum" or countries in which the asylum seeker either found protection or could reasonably have done so before arriving at his or her ultimate destination. The biggest flaw with the idea of safe country of asylum is that it has frequently been interpreted so that even a fleeting connection with a so-called safe country—transiting through a country is a common example—will be enough to remove a claim from *any* kind of consideration, despite what conditions are like in this person's country of origin and the danger this person might face there.

The second use of this term is the notion of the safe country of origin. The idea behind this policy is to provide expedited procedure to the submission of claims by nationals or residents of countries generally considered safe, and safe in this context means that neither the asylum seeker nor the group to which he or she belongs is in danger of persecution. The problem is that some of the countries that have been thought to be safe (i.e., Angola and Algeria) have been among the most violent and dangerous countries in the world.[22]

In theory, there is much to commend safe-country practices. The quicker and more efficiently we ferret out the claims of those who do not need protection, the sooner we can attend to the claims of those who are in a crisis. In practice, however, both of these safe-country notions have been disastrous for asylum seekers, and they show that the intended goal of such policies is not really establishing an orderly procedure but rather the severe reduction of asylum claims altogether.

THE STRONGEST CLAIM FOR ADMISSION

It is impossible to argue against taking in people in need of protection. That is, no matter how pressing the policy goals against the admission of refugees might seem in theory or even in practice—rising domestic unemployment, overcrowded schools, assimilation problems, and so forth—these arguments simply pale when they are compared with the life and death issues inherent in refugee protection. As the political philosopher Michael Walzer has stated: "The victims of political and religious persecution . . . make the most forceful claim for admission. 'If you don't take me in,' they say, 'I shall be killed, persecuted, brutally oppressed by the rulers of my own country.' What can we reply?"[23]

We have effectively replied this way: if we cannot defeat the principle of refugee protection, what we will do is to go after all (or nearly all) of those claiming refugee status. Which is to say that to limit the scope of our moral obligations, we have simply refused to believe that the people who have arrived at our borders are refugees.[24] This, in turn, has given rise to the widespread charge of "asylum abuse" that is heard so frequently in both Europe and the United States. While there is admittedly some abuse in the asylum application process, we have committed the gravest abuses ourselves.

AMERICAN GENEROSITY?

One reason why it is so difficult to criticize American refugee policy is that the United States has admitted about two million refugees during the course of the past two decades.[25] This is, by far, the largest number in the world—or to be accurate, the largest number in the Western world. However, one question that we never ask ourselves is whether these individuals are indeed refugees in the sense that they have a well-founded fear of persecution in their country of origin. Based on analyses that I have conducted correlating levels of political violence with refugee admissions, the data show that American refugee policy has been little more than an immigration system dressed up in humanitarian garb, in the sense that a system founded on protection from persecution addresses very little persecution.[26]

I will use the year 1994 to explain what I am talking about and to show some of the enormous deficiencies to be found in U.S. refugee policy. By this time, the Cold War had been over for five years and our former adversary, the Soviet Union (by now the Russian Republic), had been broken up into a number of independent states. Since there was no longer any Communist government to escape from, one might guess that the United States would take in very few refugees from the (former) Soviet Union (much as it had severely reduced the number of refugees from all the other Eastern bloc countries).

However, if you guessed this, you would have guessed wrong, because in terms of refugee flows from the former Soviet Union, the Cold War was not over in 1994—and, unfortunately, it is *still* not over. Of the 112,682 refugees admitted to the United States in 1994, fully 43,000 were from Russia. Did these people suffer from political persecution? Not from anything that I could see. This, however, did (and does) not matter, because under American law—the Lautenberg Amendment by name—we have very conveniently exempted certain groups of individuals from countries presently *or formerly* under Communist rule from having to show that they have personally suffered persecution.[27]

Contrast refugee admissions from Russia with refugee admissions from Rwanda that same year. You might recall that in the spring of 1994 over eight hundred thousand Rwandans were killed in one of the most horrific genocides this side of World War II. What was the American response? It was not a very good response, and it is one that we should not be particularly proud of either. Not only did the United States *not* intervene militarily to stop this slaughter as it might have, and not only did the United States take a number of steps to prevent *other* countries from intervening either, but the United States also deliberately ignored this suffering in terms of refugee protection. In 1994, the same year that the United States admitted 43,000 refugees from the democratic Russian Republic, the United States admitted a grand total of 31 (that is not a typographical error) refugees from a country where 800,000 individuals had been slaughtered. This, by the way, is no aberration. Refugee admissions from Rwanda have always been virtually nonexistent, and apparently genocide is not about to change this policy. The United States admitted all of 88 Rwandan refugees in 1995, 118 in 1996, 100 in 1997, 86 in 1998, 153 in 1999, and 345 in the year 2000.

When you think of a refugee you think of desperate flight—do you not? The prototype, of course, is the individual who has to flee his or her homeland at a moment's notice. At one time this was also true of U.S. refugee policy, but this ideal no longer comes anywhere close to describing what American refugee policy looks like now. Instead, currently upward of 80 percent of those individuals who are admitted through the U.S. overseas refugee admission program as refugees never even leave their country of origin before they travel to the United States.[28] Instead, these individuals simply go to the U.S. embassy in whatever country they happen to live in (almost invariably the Russian Republic), they apply for refugee status, then they return home and, presumably, assume normal activities awaiting notification of whether they will be admitted as a refugee to the United States.

What also adds to this immigration-like aspect of the American refugee admission system is that the refugee priority system we have created looks dangerously like the one that we have for our system of immigration, which is to say that there is a premium placed on family ties and previous work experience with an American corporation or the U.S. government itself.[29] Granted, the top priority is for individuals who are, or have been, in serious danger. However, the numbers admitted in this category have always been exceedingly small. Instead, nearly all refugees are admitted under one of the other priorities.

Another reason why I argue that the United States has had an immigration policy disguised as a refugee policy is because we do not take measures to protect those who are most vulnerable. Consider Russia once again. There are indeed individuals in Russia who are suffering from terrible levels of political persecution: civilians in the region of Chechnya who have lived through one brutal civil war and who are now in the process of trying to survive a second one. Given that the United States will admit on the order of fifteen thousand refugees from Russia this year and given that the most vulnerable group of people (by far) in all of Russia are from Chechnya, one might think that at least *some* of these refugees would be Chechens.[30] However, one would be wrong in thinking this. Instead, as a matter of course (and as a matter of politics), the United States essentially limits refugee admissions from Russia to two groups: Evangelical Christians and Jews. No doubt both of these groups face serious discrimination. However, the point is that the *discrimination* that these individuals face is nothing compared to the *persecution* that Chechen civilians face.[31]

Having commented on a number of the deficiencies that exist in American refugee policy, I should also say that there has been some improvement. I would go so far as to say that there are times when American refugee policy has almost started to resemble an actual refugee policy. Several things have been at work here. One is that the U.S. government has (finally) come to recognize that the Vietnam War is over—albeit some twenty-five years after the fact—and this has come to be reflected in the greatly diminished number of refugees from Vietnam over the past few years.[32]

A second indication of change has been the fairly dramatic rise in admissions from Africa, although one also has to point out that there was nowhere to go but up. Although Africa has the largest number of refugees in the world, it always has represented the smallest number of refugees admitted to the United States. Of the 119,317 refugees admitted to the United States in 1990, to use a typical year, only 3,490 were from the entire continent of Africa, and nearly all these refugees came from Ethiopia. By the year 2000 this number had increased fivefold to 17,549, and many more African countries were represented. Still, in a continent where there are literally millions of refugees and where the burden of meeting these protection needs invariably falls on the poorest among us, I think it is safe to say that the refugee admission policy that the United States has maintained with respect to the African continent leaves a great deal to be desired, not only from a political and legal perspective but from an ethical perspective as well.

Finally, another indication that the United States appears to be developing a bona fide system of refugee protection is that refugee admissions have now become an integral part of larger peace-building measures, although this has been limited to a few isolated places in the world, most notably Bosnia.[33] What is needed is to replicate this twofold approach in other parts of the world as well: seeking to build peace and using refugee protection as a vehicle toward that end.

TWO MILLION—BUT COMPARED TO WHAT?

As I have noted before, over the course of the past two decades the United States has admitted two million refugees, and this number is often offered as proof of the ethical nature of American foreign policy. Two million refugees sounds like a lot of refugees—it *is* a lot of refugees—but this number should not end the debate on this matter. For one thing, how many of these were truly refugees? Based on my own analysis, not many. Beyond this, it is also instructive to compare refugees against the total number of aliens lawfully admitted to the United States. Every American is familiar with the language on the base of the Statue of Liberty—give me your tired, your poor, your huddled masses yearning to be free—and this is what we have unwittingly come to think of when we think of American immigration and refugee policy.

The truth is something altogether different. Refugees (at least real refugees) are indeed the huddled masses that Emma Lazarus was talking about in her famous poem. Yet, contrary to the way in which we want to think about ourselves, the United States pays only slight attention to the world's huddled masses. Instead, for every single refugee who is admitted to the United States, about ten immigrants will gain entry. There is, of course, no law that establishes this 10:1 ratio. However, it has remained true to form for a number of years and few dare to question it.

It is important to recognize what we are doing. Immigrants are individuals who are admitted to the United States because of their family connections or because they have certain work-related skills that are needed (or at least wanted) by American business interests. However, the point is that immigrants generally are *not* people in need, while refugees are. Recall Michael Walzer's ideas earlier where he states, quite correctly, that those with the strongest claim for admission are refugees. Yet, we give a strong preference to those not in need—by a ratio of about 10 to 1—all the while pretending that the United States provides protection to the huddled masses.

THE "ETHICS" OF REFUGEE PROTECTION

There is, of course, much to be said in favor of American refugee policy. The United States, and the American people, has few ways in which it can act in a more humane and ethical manner in the world. What bothers me, however, is the combination of hypocrisy and missed opportunities. In terms of the former, in many ways we have read the refugee definition as much for our own purposes as for those in need of protection, especially in our practice of denying (our) protection to those merely fleeing war. We have also taken any number of steps to prevent individuals from being able to even apply for refugee protection in the first place. The most visible manifestation of this policy has been to intercept rafts from Haiti on the high seas and return these people back to what has been one of the most violent and brutal regimes in this hemisphere.

We have somehow rationalized our actions on the basis that our legal duties (and apparently our moral duties as well) to protect individuals arise only *after* desperate individuals have arrived in the United States. We have demanded that asylum seekers (but not quota refugees) offer proof of persecution to us that very few will be able to show, thus giving us the opportunity of denying claims when we are so disposed. And finally, our government has repeatedly questioned whether those applying for asylum in the United States have a well-founded fear of persecution, when the overwhelming majority of asylum applicants have been from some of the most violent countries in the world.[34] In short, there is a great deal of hypocrisy in American refugee policy.

The missed opportunities exist mainly in our overseas refugee protection system. Each year the United States will admit somewhere between fifty thousand and seventy-five thousand refugees from various countries in the world, although these numbers have become considerably smaller since the advent of the war on terrorism.[35] Unlike those who arrive on their own and apply for asylum (refugee status) in the United States, under the quota system the U.S. government gets to pick and choose which refugees it will offer protection to. The problem is that for years the vast majority of those who were admitted as quota refugees were simply not refugees. Rather, we have used refugee admissions as a means of fighting the Cold War—even after the Cold War has long been over. At the same time, we have systematically ignored those with the strongest need and claim for protection. In sum, there is no question that we have acted ethically in granting refugee protection. The real question is whether we have been anywhere near as ethical as we have pretended to be—or that we should be.

5

AMERiCAN ETHiCS

"Easy" Does It

Somewhere between 15 percent and 20 percent of the U.S. federal budget is spent on foreign aid; nearly three-quarters of the American people are "environmentalists," and the United States is the world's "shining city on the hill." Although the American people might not come right out and describe themselves and their country as "ethical," this is something that we fervently believe. For one thing, the American people are convinced that theirs is a *generous* nation, as evidenced by the large sums of money that this country (supposedly) spends on foreign aid each year.

The American people are also convinced that theirs is a *responsible* nation. We know that the ecosystem of this planet is quite fragile, and that is why people in this country (supposedly) have been so protective of Mother Earth. And finally, the American people are also convinced that their country is *special.* In their eyes at least, the United States serves as a beacon of hope for the rest of the world, or in the words of former president Ronald Reagan, the United States represents "the last, best hope for mankind." What we will explore in this chapter is the manner in which the American people maintain certain beliefs—sometimes in the face of a wealth of contrary evidence. The point is that it is easy for Americans to think of themselves as being ethical when they do not know better—or want to know better.

FOREIGN AID: THE MYTH OF AMERICAN GENEROSITY

In a 1995 study conducted by the University of Maryland Center for International and Security Studies and the Center for the Study of Public Attitudes, respondents were surveyed about the size and scope of American foreign aid. Although answers were all over the board, the universal theme was that the United States provided hefty sums of foreign aid. The median response was that 15 percent of the U.S. federal budget went to foreign aid. Three-quarters of the respondents were of the opinion that the amount the United States spent on foreign aid was too high (at 15 percent of the federal budget, who wouldn't think this?). When then asked what the "right" amount was, the median response was that 5 percent of the U.S. government's budget should be spent on foreign aid and that 3 percent would be too small.

This study was replicated in February 2001, and although there were some changes in public attitudes, what did not change was the delusion of generosity that we have about ourselves. Although foreign aid had actually *decreased* in relative terms during the time between the two studies, the median response in this new study had actually *increased* to 20 percent.[1]

In fact, foreign aid constitutes less than *1 percent* of the federal budget. In addition, a very large portion of this money goes to two political allies of the United States (Israel and Egypt) and very little of it goes to the poorest and the most desperate states and people in the world.[2]

In other words, almost no connection exists between the foreign aid program that the American people think their country possesses and the foreign aid program that the U.S. government actually does have. Of course, no one can really expect the public to know arcane things about the federal budget, and knowing the amount or the percentage of foreign aid in the budget would certainly qualify as being arcane. Still, it is interesting and more than coincidental that people erred high (vastly higher) rather than erring low. I would suggest that the reason for this is that the American people have this image of the United States doing good in the world, and one obvious means of doing good is by providing large amounts of foreign aid.

The point is that we do not do anywhere near as much "good" as we think we do, nor as much good as other people do. Of all the industrialized countries in the world, the United States provides the *lowest* levels of foreign aid (as a percentage of Gross Domestic Product [GDP])—actually by a long shot. While 0.15 percent of American GDP is spent on foreign aid, this compares (unfavorably) with the 0.26 percent spent by Japan, 0.37 percent spent by Germany, 0.63 percent spent by France, 0.31 percent spent by Great Britain, and 0.45 percent spent by our Canadian neighbors. Comparing American "generosity" with that of the Scandinavian countries is downright embarrassing. In 1997, per capita expenditures on foreign aid were $23 in the United States compared with $311 in Denmark.[3] Would anyone suggest that Danes are fourteen times more humanitarian— arguably, fourteen times more ethical—than Americans are? Certainly, no one in this country would do so.

Many of us have trouble with fractions, and there is also the confusion in distinguishing between the federal budget (which is the amount of money spent by our federal government) and the country's GDP (which is the worth of all the goods and services produced in a country), so let us simply use raw numbers. In 1993 the United States spent $9.72 billion on nonmilitary foreign aid. That same year Japan spent $11.26 billion, France $7.92 billion, and Germany $6.95 billion. In short, the richest and most powerful country in the world gave substantially less foreign aid than Japan did in 1993 (and in most other years), and only slightly more than France and Germany, countries that are considerably smaller than our own.

But perhaps the most fascinating and frustrating aspect of these Maryland studies is the manner in which these findings have done almost nothing to change our policies—or, apparently, our image of ourselves. Perhaps because of its novelty or maybe because of the wide discrepancy between belief and reality, the first Maryland study received a fair amount of publicity.[4]

Still, the only change in policy was that U.S. foreign aid actually *decreased* in relative terms.[5] In other words, after a study was conducted showing that the United States gave considerably less money in foreign aid than the American people think that their country gives—and considerably less money than what the American people think the United States *should* give—Congress responded by reducing these paltry amounts even further.

One thing that most certainly did not change was the image that the American people have about themselves and their country. We want to believe that ours is a generous nation; we want to believe that we are ethical people; and we want to believe that a substantial portion of our national budget is spent on foreign aid each year. And this is what we *will* believe—any and all evidence to the contrary.

THE GREEN NATION

Sometimes pollsters will ask the same question over the course of a number of years to see if there is any change in attitudes and beliefs over time. One such question that has been asked repeatedly is whether the American people would describe themselves as "environmentalists." When this question was first posed more than three decades ago, only a small percentage of the American population described themselves as such. Since then, however, there has been a steady increase, and at present somewhere around three-quarters of the American people describe themselves as environmentalists.[6] Of course, if this trend continues (and there is no reason to believe that it will not), soon virtually every man, woman, and child in this country will consider himself or herself an environmentalist.

Are Americans really environmentalists? I suppose that, in some fashion at least, this would be true. Most of us recycle regularly and take some other "environmentally friendly" measures now and then, so perhaps it is understandable why and how the public might come to view themselves this way.

The problem, however, is that there is an incredible divide between what we believe about ourselves and the reality of the collective—which is that the United States is the "dirtiest" country in the world. In terms of the production of greenhouse gases—the gases that cause global warming—the United States produces 24.3 metric tons of carbon dioxide per capita per year, compared to 4.0 for China, 13.4 for Russia, 11.6 for Germany, and 10.5 for Great Britain.[7] Per capita consumption involves another kind of American runaway. The so-called ecological footprint of an average person in the United States is 30.2 acres, compared with 15.6 acres for a German national, 3.2 acres for a Nigerian, and 2.6 acres for someone from India. In short, during his lifetime the average American consumes nearly twice as much as what an average German consumes, nearly ten times what Nigerians consume, and more than ten times what Indians consume.[8]

Like many things about the American population, this is a perfect case of cognitive dissonance: we believe something that is completely contrary to reality. In this case a substantial majority of the American population consider themselves environmentalists. But how does this square—how *can* this square?—with the horrendous environmental record of the United States? Either the quarter of the population that do not call themselves environmentalists cause most of the environmental degradation produced by the United States (not likely) or else the people in this country (all of us) should (but probably will not) come to terms with the fact that as a collective we are not anywhere near as environmentally friendly as we think we are. Or to state this more bluntly: Americans are an environmental disaster for the rest of the world.

One reason why we have never come to terms with our nation's environmental record is that we have refused to recognize this as an ethical issue.[9] Rather, environmental issues are treated as policy questions or as scientific matters, and the George W. Bush administration has gone so far as to describe the country's environmental practices in terms of the pursuit of a certain kind of "American lifestyle."[10]

The truth is that the environmental practices of the American people *are* unethical. They are unethical simply because our actions—our lifestyle choices, if you must—not only will cause harm, but they are, in large part, avoidable. Moreover, there is no recourse—no justice—for those who are victimized by our actions. Of course, our own dirty habits will eventually harm people in this country at a cost of rising ocean waters, increased and more volatile storms, and all the other predicted manifestations of global warming. However, the United States is far better placed to deal with these disasters and dislocations than other countries would be, certainly far better than a poor, low-lying country like Bangladesh that might simply disappear from the face of the earth in the next half century or so.[11] Yet, rather than playing a leading role on this issue—after all, we *are* the primary cause of these problems—the United States has done just the opposite.[12] And although the Bush administration finally acknowledged the reality of global warming in the summer of 2002, its "solution" has been a nonsolution: all we need to do is to accommodate ourselves to this new reality.[13]

But perhaps things will change and change in the oddest way. Americans like to pretend that they are environmentalists, and they do not appreciate it very much when their cover is blown. Thus, what the Bush administration has done, unwittingly or not, is to remove much of the hypocrisy. Americans *do* seem to think that they have a God-given right to live the lifestyle they want, environmental considerations be damned. Still, nobody wants this stated publicly. The same thing is also true for the Kyoto Protocol. This international treaty was negotiated while Bill Clinton was president, and it is intended to substantially reduce the levels of greenhouse gases in the atmosphere by setting targets that the industrialized countries are supposed to meet. However, rather than decreasing the levels of greenhouse gases, U.S. emissions rose by some 18 percent between 1990 and 2000.[14] Unfortunately, very few viewed this as a problem, and the reason for this is that it is apparently more important to pose as an environmentalist, as opposed to truly being an environmentalist. And so nary a dissenting word was heard.

What the Bush administration has done wrong, perhaps, is to end the charade that the American people have been living with. While the United States was a part of the Kyoto process, we all could pretend that the United States was deeply concerned with addressing the emission of greenhouse gases. The Bush administration has now exposed our country's cover—and Americans do not seem particularly happy that their country can no longer pretend to be something that it is not: environmentally friendly.

THE "SHINING CITY ON THE HILL"

In 1630 Massachusetts Bay governor John Winthrop declared that "wee shall be as a Citty upon a Hill, the eies of all people are upon us."[15] Update the language and fast forward several hundred years to Ronald Reagan's acceptance speech at the 1980 Republican Convention, and the only change in this thinking is that an adjective has been added: the United States is now "the Shining City on the Hill."

The sentiment being expressed, of course, is that we are one of the "good guys." Through divine intervention or the forces of history or whatever, we are on the side of what is right and what is good. The American people believe this as strongly as they believe anything. According to one survey, fully 81 percent of the people in this country believe that the United States has a "special role" in the world—and my guess is that the other 19 percent were not exactly telling the truth.[16]

The truth is an altogether different matter. What we systematically, conveniently, and immorally ignore is the manner in which the United States has been allied with some of the nastiest and most violent regimes in the world, and thus complicit in the atrocities that have been carried out in those countries.[17] Much of the talk before the latest war with Iraq was on the necessity of "regime change" in that country. Yet, regime change has long been a part of American foreign policy. The problem is that many of the regimes that the United States has worked toward changing have been democratic governments. In addition, rather than aligning ourselves with the poor, the downtrodden, and the dispossessed in other countries, the U.S. government has done just the opposite, although this has never made a dent in the public consciousness in this country.

What follows is an alphabet (almost) of countries where the United States has engaged in nefarious practices and supported brutal and corrupt military dictatorships. Let me apologize at the outset for the length of this list, but it is not my doing. Actually, it *is* my doing, and the doing of everybody else in this country. Most remarkable of all is how we have failed to understand this.

A

Angola: Somewhere between five hundred thousand and one million civilians were killed during the course of Angola's horrendous decades-long civil war that appears to have ended in 2002. Throughout the 1980s and into the 1990s, Jonas Savimbi, the leader of the revolutionary force UNITA, was the golden boy of conservative Republicans. However, after the Cold War ended, Savimbi was no longer of any use to the United States, although he continued to make a career out of violating human rights and ceasefires alike. In a commentary on his death in spring 2002, columnist Nicholas Kristof provides the perfect description of Savimbi: "Our Own Terrorist."[18]

Argentina: The U.S. government was a staunch ally of the various Argentine military dictatorships that conducted that country's "Dirty War" from 1976 until the early 1980s, in which more than ten thousand civilians were killed.[19] Despite the obvious brutality of these military regimes—one of the government's favorite methods of killing dissidents was to throw them out of airplanes—the Reagan administration maintained that the Argentine government was deserving of U.S. support because it was "authoritarian" and not "totalitarian" in nature.

B

Brazil: In 1964, the U.S. government gave the green light to a military coup that overthrew the civilian government of Joao Goulart, a progressive nationalist intent on instituting various schemes for land, education, and labor reform. The United States then aligned itself with the military dictatorships that ruled Brazil. Although all of this was (and still is) completely lost on the American public, it certainly did not go unnoticed in Brazil. As Lawrence Weschsler writes:

> The *Brasil: Nunca Más* [a report on torture practices in Brazil] authors hold the United States co-responsible to a significant

degree for the doctrine of national security, its imposition on Brazil in the 1964 coup, and the growing use and increasingly effective organization of torture in Brazil thereafter.[20]

C

Cambodia: By violating Cambodian neutrality and dragging this country into the larger Vietnam War, the United States played a key role in setting in motion what eventually became the most massive genocide in history, where between one-quarter and one-third of the population was simply eliminated.[21] William Shawcross ends his book *Sideshow: Kissinger, Nixon and the Destruction of Cambodia* with these observations about the role of the United States:

> In Cambodia, the imperatives of a small and vulnerable people were consciously sacrificed to the interests of strategic design. For this reason alone the design was flawed—sacrifice the parts and what becomes of the whole? The country was used to practice ill-conceived theories and to fortify a notion of American credibility that could in fact only be harmed by such actions. Neither the United States nor its friends nor those who are caught helplessly in its embrace are well served when its leaders act, as Nixon and Kissinger acted, without care. Cambodia was not a mistake; it was a crime. The world is diminished by the experience.[22]

Chile: There is little doubt that the United States sought to have Salvador Allende, the Socialist president of Chile, removed from office after he was elected in 1970. Or to quote the immortal words of Secretary of State Henry Kissinger, there was no reason why Chile should be allowed to "go Communist due to the irresponsibility of its own people." The coup finally took place on another September 11 (1973), and there is evidence of a substantial American role in this operation.[23] Publicly, the U.S. government maintained "cordial" relations with the Pinochet military dictatorship, and Congress attempted to punish the Chilean government.[24] However, behind the scenes the United States maintained very close ties with the

Pinochet dictatorship, and it pushed forward and cooperated with Operation Condor—a cross-border operation of assassination, abduction, torture, and intimidation carried out by the military regimes ruling Chile, Argentina, Uruguay, and Paraguay.

Colombia: For the past few decades the United States has supported what it calls a war on drugs in Colombia, while the reality is that American habits and policies are supporting a brutal civil war between various guerrilla factions and paramilitary and security forces. Robin Kirk, an analyst for Human Rights Watch (a nongovernmental organization), has described the role that the United States has played in the disintegration of Colombian life in these terms:

> Our pleasures are tearing Colombia apart. Our leisure funds terror. Our parties pull Colombia under, as surely as a stone sinks cloth in water. Our addictions and experimentations ensnare not just ourselves and our families, but a nation. Most of all, our unwillingness to acknowledge our behavior and examine its real consequences threatens to sink Colombia.[25]

Cyprus: There is strong evidence that the United States worked with the Greek military dictatorship in removing President Makarios of Cyprus from office in 1974. This, in turn, led to a brutal Turkish invasion and to the island's partition that remains to this day. Describing National Security Advisor and U.S. Secretary of State Kissinger's role in the coup, Christopher Hitchens writes:

> Using covert channels, and short-circuiting the democratic processes in his own country, he made himself a silent accomplice in a plan of political assassination, and when this plan went awry, it led to the deaths of thousands of civilians, the violent uprooting of almost 200,000 refugees, and the creation of an unjust and unstable amputation of Cyprus that constitutes a serious threat to peace a full quarter of a century later.[26]

D

Dominican Republic: Democratically elected President Juan Bosch was overthrown in a military coup in 1963. While in

office, Bosch had fathered a new constitution that limited foreign acquisition of Dominican land, provided for profit sharing
for agricultural workers, and required owners of land in
excess of certain broad limits to sell the excess or distribute it
to landless farmers. These constitutional reforms were eliminated immediately after Bosch was removed from office. In
1965 when a civil uprising "threatened" to return Bosch to his
rightful position, U.S. Marines invaded the country and prevented this from taking place.

E

East Timor: Indonesia invaded this former Portuguese colony
the day after U.S. president Gerald Ford and secretary of state
Kissinger met with Indonesian military officials in Jakarta
and gave a "green light" to this operation.[27] Upward of two
hundred thousand civilians were killed during the course of
the invasion and the quarter century of occupation of East
Timor.[28] Throughout this entire time, the United States provided military and political support to the Indonesian government.

El Salvador: The United States was intimately involved in this
country's civil war that lasted from 1979 to December 31,
1991, bringing about the deaths of some seventy-five thousand civilians.[29] Notwithstanding the atrocities carried out by
the Salvadoran military and paramilitary forces, the only time
U.S. support for the Salvadoran government seemed to
weaken was in 1980 when four American churchwomen were
raped and murdered, and in 1989 when six Jesuit priests
were killed in a university dormitory. Mark Danner's book *The
Massacre at El Mozote* provides an extraordinary account of
just one example of American complicity and duplicity in the
horrors of El Salvador.[30]

G

Greece: It is still not clear whether the United States master-
minded the military coup in April 1967 that ended democratic

governance in this country. However, what is certain is that the Lyndon B. Johnson administration quickly embraced the Papadopoulus regime and that relations between the military junta and the United States became even closer during the Nixon presidency.[31] President Clinton issued an apology for these American actions during a trip to Greece in November 1999.

Guatemala: The United States directed and actively participated in the military coup that removed the popularly elected president, Jacobo Arbenz, from office in 1954. The slaughter of Communist "sympathizers" began almost immediately, at the behest of, and under the direction of, U.S. government officials, and during the course of the next four decades upward of two hundred thousand civilians would be killed. The United States also helped to turn the Guatemalan army into the most brutal military in the hemisphere.[32] Guatemala is the only other country (besides Greece) where the United States has issued an unequivocal apology for its complicity in repression. This issue is explored more fully in chapter 6.

H

Haiti: U.S. involvement in Haiti goes back a long way. It includes the American occupation of this country from 1915 to 1934 as well as the decades of support for the father–son dictatorship team of "Papa Doc" (1957–1971) and then "Baby Doc" (1971–1986) Duvalier. Not only did the United States support repressive regimes in Haiti, but through its interdiction program, it has gone to great lengths to prevent refugees from fleeing to the United States.

Honduras: Honduras has served as a useful training site for U.S. military operations in Central America, first, in the U.S.-led overthrow of Guatemalan president Arbenz in 1954 and, later, during the 1980s as the main training site for Nicaraguan Contra rebels. These actions served to militarize Honduras in a number of ways, most notably by equipping and training members of the Battalion 3–16 death squads. As American influence in that country expanded, the human rights situation in Honduras steadily deteriorated.[33]

I

Indonesia: The United States first worked toward the elimination of the Indonesian independence leader Achmad Sukarno in 1958, but these efforts did not come to fruition until a U.S.-backed military coup in 1965, which resulted in a nationwide bloodbath. Jonathan Kwitny writes:

> [W]e know these things for certain: U.S. military, intelligence, economic, and administrative experts immediately flocked to Indonesia and began reorganizing things. The generals, with the advice of U.S. government agents but hardly against their inclinations, had the army begin a massive elimination of communist sympathizers throughout Indonesia. Estimates of the number killed have ranged from a low of 300,000 to a high of 1 million.[34]

In addition, as mentioned earlier, President Ford and Secretary of State Kissinger supported the Indonesian government's invasion of East Timor.

Iran: Concerned about the possibilities that the Iranian government might nationalize the country's oil industries, in 1953 the United States was an active participant in the overthrow of Premier Mohammed Mossadegh, placing in power the Shah of Iran.[35] The Shah was a particularly brutal ruler, and his secret police organization (SAVAK) routinely tortured political dissidents. Because of his staunch anti-Communist stance, however, the Shah remained one of America's greatest friends. In early 1979, the Shah stepped down from power in the face of a nationwide movement against his Western and brutal ways. When the Shah was admitted to the United States for medical treatment in November 1979, Iranian "students" took hostage a group of American embassy personnel (some of whom were CIA operatives), and what ensued was an extraor-

dinarily tense 444-day standoff between the two countries
and an enmity that continues to this day.

Iraq: For some time, former Iraqi dictator Saddam Hussein was
the #1 enemy of the United States. This, however, was not
always the case. In fact, the United States not only supported
Iraq during the Iran–Iraq War in the 1980s, but it deliberately
ignored the atrocities carried out by the Iraqi government,
including the chemical gassing of civilian (Kurdish) populations.[36] Beyond this, from the period between the end of the
Persian Gulf War (1991) and the start of the war on Iraq
(2003), American-led economic sanctions caused the deaths
of some 350,000 Iraqi children. Finally, more than ten thousand Iraqi civilians have been killed during the course of the
ongoing war in Iraq.

Israel: Israel has no closer ally than the United States. For decades Israel has been the largest recipient of U.S. foreign aid
(although Israel is anything but a developing country), and for
just as long the United States has protected Israel from cen-
sure before any number of international forums. Because of
this alliance, the United States has been willing to overlook
Israel's illegal occupation of Palestinian lands, the systematic
torture of Palestinian suspects, and the purposeful killing of
Palestinian supporters.

K

Korea (South): Between October 1948 and February 1949,
upward of thirty thousand people were killed in the Jeju Massacre that was carried out to "eliminate" those who had boy-
cotted national elections and thus were thought to be
Communist sympathizers.[37] Yang Ju Hoon, a prime ministe-
rial appointee who heads a committee established to collect
testimony about the massacre, believes that American military and political leaders were aware of these killings and perhaps had ordered them.[38] Beyond this, the U.S. government
actively supported each of the military dictatorships that
ruled the country from the end of World War II until 1993.

L

Laos: It is estimated that approximately thirty thousand Hmong tribesmen were killed during the CIA-led war in that country and another ten thousand after the U.S. government abandoned Laos. In his disturbing book *Shooting at the Moon*, Roger Warner writes of the manner in which the United States used Laos (and Laotians) for larger geopolitical ends relating to the Vietnam War: "America ended up sacrificing the tribals and the lowland Laotians for U.S. goals in Vietnam. These allies, or proxies, were abandoned once the war [Vietnam] was over, and the results were a permanent stain on America's reputation."[39] He continues: "[T]he United States had used the tribals for nothing. The Hmong hadn't been able to save Laos, and nothing tried in Laos was able to salvage the American effort in South Vietnam. The whole thing had been futile, a delusion."[40]

N

Nicaragua: The United States has had a long and contentious relationship with Nicaragua going all the way back to 1858 when William Walker, a soldier of fortune from Tennessee, declared himself president of Nicaragua—and his new government was immediately recognized by the United States! From the mid-1930s to 1979, American policy was essentially to prop up the Somoza father–son dictatorships. Of Somoza Garcia, the elder, to use the immortal words of Franklin Roosevelt, "he may be a son of a bitch but . . . he's *our* son of a bitch," and thus it was necessary for the United States to keep him in power. Much the same was true of Somoza Debayle, the son whose dictatorship we actively supported from 1956 (after his father had been assassinated) to 1979 when a group calling themselves Sandinistas removed him from power. For more than a decade thereafter, the United States sought to have the Sandinistas removed from power—to "cry uncle" in the words of Ronald Reagan—by supporting the Contras, an especially violent counterrevolutionary group.

P

Panama: For many years the United States supported the corrupt drug-running practices of Panamanian strongman General Manuel Noriega. The reason for this is that Noriega was a staunch anti-Communist. Only when the war on Communism conflicted with other U.S. goals, most notably the war on drugs, was Noriega viewed as being expendable.[41] When he refused to leave quietly, the United States invaded Panama in order to place him under arrest. During the course of the invasion, anywhere from several hundred to several thousand civilians were killed.

Paraguay: The United States actively supported General Alfredo Stroessner throughout his thirty-five-year dictatorship. It did so by providing not only military aid, but also information about the regime's enemies that was used to "neutralize" (i.e., murder) these opponents. Archives unearthed in 1999 showed that U.S. military officials were instrumental in creating Stroessner's police state.[42]

Philippines: Few people remember (or seem to want to remember) that the Philippines is a former American colony. The Filipino War of Independence at the turn of last century was one of the bloodiest in history—estimates are that one-sixth of the population (or one million people) were killed—in what ultimately was an unsuccessful effort to obtain independence from the United States.[43] More recently, for decades the United States supported the brutal and corrupt rule of Ferdinand Marcos even after Marcos had declared martial law in 1972. Raymond Bonner has described American policy during that time as "waltzing with a dictator."[44] Only after Marcos blatantly stole the presidential election in 1986 did the United States cut ties with him, and he immediately fell from power.

R

Rwanda: The crime we committed in Rwanda was doing nothing in the face of genocide in 1994 that resulted in the deaths of over eight hundred thousand people in the space of a few short weeks. Worse than that, the United States actively blocked other countries from intervening as well. Philip Gourevitch's account deserves to be quoted at length:

> The desertion of Rwanda by UN forces was Hutu Power's greatest diplomatic victory to date, and it can be credited almost single-handedly to the United States. With the memory of the Somalia debacle still very fresh, the White House had just finished drafting a document called Presidential Decision Directive 25, which amounted to a checklist of reasons to avoid American military involvement in UN peacekeeping missions. It hardly mattered that Dallaire's [the head of the United Nations Assistance Mission in Rwanda] call for an expanded force and mandate would not have required American troops, or that the mission was not properly peacekeeping, but genocide prevention. PDD 25 also contained what Washington policymakers call "language" urging that the United States should persuade others not to undertake the missions that it wished to avoid. In fact, the Clinton administration's ambassador to the UN, Madeleine Albright, opposed leaving even the skeleton crew of two hundred seventy in Rwanda. Albright went on to become Secretary of State, largely because of her reputation as a "daughter of Munich," a Czech refugee from Nazism with no tolerance for appeasement and with a taste for projecting U.S. force abroad to bring rogue dictators and criminal states to heel. Her name is rarely associated with Rwanda, but ducking and pressuring others to duck, as the death toll leapt from thousands to tens of thousands to hundreds of thousands, was the absolute low point in her career as a stateswoman.[45]

S

South Africa: Throughout the 1980s, U.S. policy toward South Africa was termed constructive engagement. The premise behind this policy was that the white majority regime in South Africa would be long-lived, and that the black majority was essentially irrelevant to the "national interest" of the United States. In addition, the United States allied itself with the various wars the South African government was fighting in this region, most notably the war in Angola.[46]

T

Turkey: Throughout the 1990s, the Turkish government waged what was arguably a genocidal war against the Kurdish population in the southeastern part of the country. As a result, some 2.5 million villagers were displaced and more than twenty-three thousand people were killed. Nearly all the weaponry used in this war was provided by the United States, as domestic considerations—most notably jobs in the American arms industry—took precedence over any and all human rights considerations.[47]

U

Uruguay: Formerly known as the "Switzerland of Latin America" because of its long history of democratic rule, Uruguay suffered massive levels of repression from the early 1970s to 1985. Of a population in 1970 of three million people, somewhere between three hundred thousand and four hundred thousand went into exile during the next decade and a half. Of those remaining, one in every fifty was detained at one time or another for interrogation; and one in every five hundred received a long prison sentence for political offenses. (Comparable figures in the United States would have involved the emigration of nearly thirty million individuals, the detention of five million, and extended incarceration of over five hundred thousand.) Regarding the relationship between the United States and the Uruguayan military dictatorship, Lawrence Weschler writes:

> The United States was nowhere near as deeply and directly involved in the final subversion of Uruguay's democracy as it had been in the case of Brazil's, or would be, later that same year, in the case of Chile's. Nor did the United States provide the Uruguayan military with massive military assistance following the coup. . . . What the U.S. Department of State did lavish upon Uruguay all through the early seventies were excuses—public assurances that all the repression going on down there was merely a temporary response to an immediate

emergency. And before that, what the United States had equipped Uruguay's military with was doctrinal justification.[48]

V

Vietnam: All that most Americans know about the Vietnam War is that more than fifty-five thousand American soldiers were killed during the course of hostilities. Apparently, this is as far as our morality extends. What we have chosen to ignore is that more than three million Vietnamese (mainly civilians) were killed in the war as well. And because of the widespread use of chemical defoliants such as Agent Orange, the Vietnamese people continue to live (and die) with the consequences of the war.

Z

Zaire/Congo: The United States has a long and sordid track record in Zaire/Congo. As the country was emerging from Belgian colonial rule, the U.S. government determined that the new country's young, dynamic leader, Patrice Lumumba, was too "socialist," and forces associated with the CIA assassinated him.[49] Subsequently, the United States was able to place its man, Colonel Joseph Mobutu, into power. Kwitny comments on the "transition": "The fledgling Congolese leaders, so desperately needing an example to follow, were being instructed by the world's leading proponent of liberty and democracy on how a political system ought to work: you kill your legally elected rivals and seize power."[50] Mainly through the support of the United States, Mobutu ruled for more than three decades. When he was finally removed from office in 1997, he was considered one of the five richest men in the world—thanks to the U.S. government and American taxpayers.

AMERICAN "EXCEPTIONALISM"—AND AMERICA'S VALUES

What I have tried to do in this chapter is to show that American "exceptionalism" is, in large part, a figment of our collective imagination. We are nowhere near as generous as we think we are. Rather, in terms of foreign aid the American people would actually hold the title of being the *least* generous people in the industrialized world. We are not the environmentalists so many of us claim to be. In fact, no people in the world cause anywhere near the amount of damage to the planet that Americans do. Finally, we are nowhere close to being as "good" and as "righteous" as we so fervently believe we are. Instead, America's friends and allies read like a Who's Who of brutal dictatorships: Pinochet, Noriega, Savimbi, Somoza (father and son), Mobutu, Stroessner, Duvalier (father and son), Marcos, and Suharto—the list is unimaginably long. In short, America the Beautiful is not nearly as beautiful—or as ethical—as the people in this country think it is. And yet the American people cannot seem to fathom why so many people hate the United States.

Will any of this change? It might, but a number of things are working against this. For one thing, myths of American exceptionalism are deeply ingrained in our national psyche. And has there ever been a politician (other than Jimmy Carter)[51] who has had the temerity to even hint that the United States has not lived up to its image or its promise?

Beyond the myths and the national grandstanding, what will also prevent us from taking any stock of our actions in the world is that it is not common to consider the matters discussed in this chapter as constituting ethical issues. Rather, we live in some kind of strange and perverse world in which our population can easily recognize some ethical issues as ethical issues (i.e., stealing from the coffee fund at work), while at the same time we have been trained to believe that such things as supporting genocide in Guatemala or Turkey; removing democratically elected officials in Brazil or Indonesia or Chile or Zaire; or choking the world on our pollution (somehow) do not constitute ethical issues. And I am afraid that until *this* changes, we will be fated to continue our present policies—and "others" will be fated to suffer the consequences of these policies as well.

Yet, there are some indications that this blind and arrogant view toward the world could be changing. In part II we examine several phenomena that give some indication that ethical standards in this country have been in the process of being transformed. However, the national tragedy of September 11 could easily derail all these moral advances, and we return to this in the concluding chapter.

II

CODA OF HOPE?

6

FACiNG OUR PAST

We live in the Age of Apology. Within just the past few years, a number of states have apologized for "wrongs" that they have committed—either within their own domestic realm[1] or against people in other lands.[2] The Pope has issued several noteworthy and moving apologies for some of the sins of the Catholic Church.[3] Even corporations and civic organizations have started to examine their own past actions. For example, Aetna Life has issued an apology for previously carrying insurance on slaves, while the *Hartford Courant* newspaper has apologized for running advertisements of slave sales.[4]

The focus of this chapter is on state apologies (American apologies in particular), and on one level, at least, it is easy to see why they engender so much cynicism.[5] For one thing, given the enormity of some of the crimes for which state apologies have been issued—slavery,[6] certain aspects of colonial rule,[7] and complicity in genocide[8] just for starters—*any* attempt "to come to terms" with such a past, not only will *seem* lacking, but of necessity *will be* lacking. More than that, however, the manner in which so many apologies have been given would easily lead to this jaundiced view. Almost without exception, state apologies have given every appearance of being an insincere affair. Which is to say that a few soft and somber words have been uttered about how wrong and how misguided some previous policies or actions had been. But after going on record acknowledging some particular horror from the past, every effort is then made to get through the apology as quickly and as painlessly as possible.

Yet, neither the cacophony of proffered apologies nor the deficiencies to be found in so many of them should obscure their possible importance and meaning. The ultimate question is whether state apologies represent any kind of fundamental change, not simply in the practices of states but in the relationships between states and between peoples. Among other things, it is noteworthy that strong states are apologizing to the people of weak states. It might be that this relative strength gives such states license to utter some meaningless words concerning wrongs from the past—or perhaps something else is going on.

I believe that the apology phenomenon is (or at least could be) of enormous importance. As I will explain here, by apologizing, we are not only recognizing the humanity in "others," but we are also recognizing the inhumanity in ourselves. This is no small feat. Beyond that, however, by apologizing we are also repudiating the ethical standards that allowed this kind of behavior to arise in the first place. But unlike those who see these apologies as a smug way of making ourselves feel superior to those before us, I see this as a very strong indication that we consider our *present* moral standards to be lacking as well. And the apology is (or, again, could be) an important first step toward constructing a much different moral framework.

Despite the novelty and the importance of these apologies, I think we have not apologized well, as I explain in much of what follows. Part of the problem is that this really is virgin territory in the sense that there has been little precedent for this kind of thing. Thus, although many of these "crimes" occurred some time ago, this is the first time that governments are apologizing for these wrongs.

But it is more than inexperience. The truth is that we do not know *how* to apologize, which is a reflection of the fact that we still do not know *what* we should be apologizing for. What we do know is that some part of our history has a rancid smell to it. And for this we are sorry or at least appear to be sorry. However, being human (after all) we also do not want our lives disrupted very much. And so what we have done is to make some rather halfhearted attempts at apologizing for a few of our past misdeeds. We might think that this is good enough but it is not, or at least not good enough if we are serious about wanting to be ethical beings and to live in an ethical country. It also has to be said that our efforts to date will not be good enough for other people either. Thus, rather than healing old wounds, our incomplete efforts might well have the opposite effect. If we truly do want to come to terms not only with our past but with ourselves, we are going to have to address our wrongs in a much more serious and systematic way than we have to date. What follows is how this might be accomplished.

AMERICAN APOLOGIES

No country has issued more apologies to more people than the United States has.[9] Within the domestic realm, the U.S. government has apologized for the internment of Japanese Americans during World War II;[10] for the so-called Tuskegee experiment in which a group of poor, Southern black men was purposely left untreated so that scientific researchers could study the effects of syphilis; and for the U.S. government's involvement in the removal of the Hawaiian monarchy in 1893.[11]

As we have seen throughout this book, it is much easier to maintain consistent ethical standards within a domestic setting and much more difficult to do so (and have an interest in doing so) once we go beyond our country's territorial boundaries. In this respect, then, it has been our apologies to others—what I will call transnational state apologies—that in many respects are far more noteworthy. To date, the United States has apologized to the people of Greece for American support of the military junta that ruled that country from 1967 to 1974.[12] The U.S. government also has issued an apology (of sorts) to the people of Rwanda for not intervening and not taking steps to halt the genocide in that country in 1994.[13] And during President Bill Clinton's same trip to Africa in 1998 (what some have called his contrition tour), the United States issued a general apology for

the way in which American national security interests domi-
nated U.S. policy toward Africa during the Cold War.[14]

Rather than focusing on any or all of these, the apology I will
focus on is the apology to the Guatemalan people issued by Clinton during a state visit to that country in spring 1999. The apology was in large part a reaction to the findings of an independent
Guatemalan truth commission that had tied the United States
to the genocidal practices of the Guatemalan military. The apology, in its entirety, was as follows:

> For the United States it is important that I state clearly that sup-
> port for military forces and intelligence units which engaged in
> violence and widespread repression was wrong, and the United
> States must not repeat that mistake. We must, and we will,
> instead, continue to support the peace and reconciliation process
> in Guatemala.[15]

To my mind the apology is a combination of what is both good
and bad about transnational state apologies. The good is easier
to see: the United States is publicly acknowledging and apologizing for being in bed with some pretty awful characters in Guatemala. The following is a list of the deficiencies:

Publicity. Even though Clinton was publicly acknowledging
active American involvement in a war in which upward of two
hundred thousand civilians were killed, tens of thousands more
were arrested and tortured, and over a million people were displaced,[16] the apology to Guatemala was met by an enormous collective yawn—at least in the United States. Although the
metropolitan edition of the *New York Times* had a front-page
story on the apology,[17] the national edition ran its story on page
12.[18] Only one television network (CNN) ever made any mention
of the apology.[19] Of course, Clinton could not have dictated television and newspaper coverage. Still, the manner in which the
apology was delivered, particularly its extreme brevity, might
well have given a strong indication that the issue was not considered to be a particularly pressing one, especially to the audience
back home.

This, in turn, leads to the related issue of the apology's

intended audience. The apology was directed at the Guatemalan people and, to a lesser extent, the current Guatemalan government. Still, what is not clear is why Clinton made no serious effort to include and engage the American people. The admitted wrongs were committed by the U.S. government but on behalf of the citizens of this country. The apology as well was issued by the U.S. government but on behalf of the citizens of this country. There is no reason, then, why the president could not also have spoken *to* the American people at the same time that he was speaking *for* them. This is particularly the case when one considers how little the U.S. public knows about international events—even (perhaps especially) with respect to the manner in which the United States operates in the world.[20]

Ceremony. An apology should be a solemn occasion, accompanied by special ceremonies befitting such an event. For the U.S. government's apology for the Tuskegee experiment,[21] for example, the eight remaining survivors were invited to the White House where the government's apology was issued in what press reports described as a very emotional ceremony.[22] And perhaps the most noteworthy, and certainly the most memorable, state apology was West German chancellor Willy Brandt's unscripted genuflection at the Warsaw Ghetto.[23]

Unfortunately, the apology to Guatemala had none of the trappings to indicate that an event of any great significance was taking place. There was no attempt to address the Guatemalan people and the American public by television or by radio address. Essentially, there was no special ceremony at all. Instead, Clinton's apology was issued as part of some opening remarks at a roundtable discussion on peace efforts in Guatemala.

Explanation. Related to this, one of the biggest shortcomings of the Guatemalan apology is that it provides virtually no detail as to what the apology is for, and this dearth of information in the apology also helps to explain why the event received so little attention in the United States. Thus, the apology makes no mention of the way in which one U.S. corporation—United Fruit— came to completely dominate political and economic life in Guatemala for nearly a century.[24] The apology provides no indication of the manner in which the U.S. government was deeply involved in overthrowing Jacobo Arbenz, the popularly elected president of Guatemala. What was Arbenz's crime? In the early 1950s as Guatemala was only starting to emerge from its feudal past, President Arbenz attempted a modest land reform proposal that was disfavored by foreign (read *American*) investors, and he also sought to institute a social welfare program that focused on illiteracy. *And for this*, Arbenz was violently thrown out of office in a 1954 coup that was both engineered by and (to a lesser extent) carried out by agents of the U.S. government.[25] And the bloodbath that was to engulf Guatemala for the next four decades began immediately, as eight thousand peasants were murdered within the first month of the coup—at the behest of, and through the direction of, the U.S. government.[26]

In his two-sentence apology, Clinton spoke of U.S. "support" for Guatemalan military forces. However, this grossly underestimates the American role in almost single-handedly transforming a ragtag constabulary force into one of the most efficient and brutal militaries in the world,[27] and it decidedly underplays the decisive role played by U.S. involvement in the decades-long civil war.[28] In addition, in this briefest of apologies Clinton does not even acknowledge what already has been documented by U.S. security agencies: that the United States placed on its own payroll some of Guatemala's worst human rights abusers as so-called intelligence assets.[29]

In short, in stark contrast to something like the apology issued by the Canadian government to its aboriginal population, which was based on an exhaustive catalog of state abuses,[30] the U.S. apology to Guatemala says very little about the particulars for why an apology was being issued in the first place. Is there any wonder, then, that the apology had so little impact on the American public and on the U.S. political system?

Financial Assistance. At the time that the apology was issued, Clinton made note that the United States had contributed $1.5 million to support the work of the Guatemalan truth commission, and that there were plans to provide $25 million to support the country's peace accords through aid to the judicial sector, to education, to literacy training, to the generation of income, and to citizen participation in government.[31] While such measures are commendable enough, it also has to be noted that these amounts are nowhere close to the hundreds of millions if not billions of dollars spent by the United States in the course of committing these now-acknowledged wrongs. Perhaps there is much to be learned in this regard from state apologies (and even near apologies) within the domestic realm where wide-ranging assistance schemes have become a more integral part of dealing with the past.

Justice.   Another shortcoming of the apology to Guatemala is that it was devoid of any justice. Thus, notwithstanding the president's public admission that wrongs had been committed, there is no prospect that a single U.S. official will be held accountable—although many of the American officials who carried out these wrongs are still alive, and perhaps some are still working for the federal bureaucracy or in the military or for a security agency. Who, for example, was responsible for placing known human rights abusers on the payroll of the U.S. government?[32] And to what extent were American officials present while atrocities were carried out?[33]

Consistency.   A broader problem relates to the countries where apologies have been given—but also the countries where apologies have *not* been given. In terms of transnational apologies, to date the U.S. government has issued an unequivocal apology to only two governments (Guatemala and Greece), a general apology for not doing the right thing in Africa during the Cold War, and a quasi-apology to Rwanda for not intervening to prevent the genocide in that country in 1994.

But this raises the question of why these apologies and not others. Clinton visited El Salvador immediately before his trip to Guatemala where he issued the apology under discussion. However, Clinton refrained from apologizing to the people of El Salvador. What, exactly, differentiates U.S. activity in Guatemala from U.S. activity in El Salvador? In both countries the United States supported anti-Communist governments, and in both countries these governments carried out widespread human rights abuses against civilian populations.[34] As a result of these repressive policies, upward of two hundred thousand civilians were killed in Guatemala and an estimated seventy-five thousand civilians were killed in El Salvador. The question, once again, is this: what differentiates these two countries so that an apology is warranted in one case but not in the other? Could it be the number of people who were killed? If not, what does? There is also the matter of how and why there has been a state apology to the people of Greece and not in many other states where there were much greater levels of U.S. involvement and where human rights atrocities were far greater (see the alphabetical listing in the chapter 5).

Understanding.   Related to this, perhaps the most important question that the party issuing an apology can ask itself is "why" it did what it did. Without this, the apology will do little to advance understanding, leaving the apologizer to commit the same kinds of mistakes and the same kinds of wrongs over and over again—and leaving those who already have been victimized in a position where they (and others) might well be harmed again in the future.

The problem with the apology to Guatemala, as noted before, is that it does not provide any particular insight into U.S. activities in Guatemala. In that way, then, the apology itself does little to advance any understanding of the relationship between these two countries. Yet, perhaps the apology to Guatemala accomplishes something more than this. What this apology does is to establish the principle that the blanket justification—fighting Communism—that the U.S. government and the American people have allowed themselves to give for the past half century is simply not going to be sufficient anymore. Rather, what this apology clearly establishes is the idea that while opposing the totalitarian strains in Communist regimes might well have been a noble goal, it did not (and it does not) justify any and all American activities in pursuit of that end.

But this has to be pushed even further. How is it that the "world's leading democracy" was so intolerant of democratic impulses in other countries? Why has the United States repeatedly sided with the rich and the powerful and opposed the aspirations of the poor and the oppressed in so many countries, not simply just in Guatemala? And finally, how and why has the United States backed so many murderous regimes? A proper apology would begin a meaningful national debate on such questions, and the American people would thereby learn a great deal about their country and about themselves. Unfortunately, no apology has come even remotely close to achieving this. However, it also has to be said that no apology has been designed to achieve this goal either.[35]

Forgiveness.   One of the problems with state apologies is that the power imbalance that gave rise to the wrongful act is oftentimes perpetuated even in the process where amends are supposedly being made. The powerful state not only decides if and when an apology will be given (or whether a near apology will be provided instead) but also decides the manner in which all this will be done. The receiving state—and its victimized people— invariably has the apology dictated to it.

A much better approach would be for the state that has committed wrongs (the United States in our present discussion) to *ask* the aggrieved state (on behalf of its people) for forgiveness.[36] In this way, the wronged party is put in a position of exercising some measure of authority in the matter. Perhaps the receiving state would question the sincerity of the other state and decide that it will not grant forgiveness. Or perhaps the victimized people (through their state) would conclude that the restitution scheme that has been offered is insufficient. The receiving state would now be in a much stronger position to demand changes than it would be in the situation where the apologizing state controls the tone and the terms of the apology.

Hypocrisy.   An apology is a promise to change behavior. A very strong indication that an apology is insincere is if the same behavior continues. The apology to Guatemala states that "support for military forces and intelligence units which engaged in violence and widespread repression was wrong, and the United States must not repeat that mistake." The question, then, is whether the United States *has* repeated this mistake. For example, after issuing the apology to Guatemala, the United States continued to arm and equip a Turkish military that was carrying out gross and systematic human rights abuses against Kurdish populations in the southeastern part of Turkey.[37] Instead of halting these practices, as the apology would dictate, arms sales to Turkey continued apace. And rather than apologizing for U.S. involvement in these human rights violations, the best that Clinton could do during a state visit to Turkey in November 1999 was to quietly hint to his Turkish hosts that they might want to pay closer attention to human rights concerns.[38]

In sum, the apology to Guatemala says very little, it helps us to understand very little, and, perhaps, it changes very little. That said, however, what is needed is a serious attempt to build on this effort. First, there needs to be a far more systematic effort at cataloging U.S. wrongs, not simply in Guatemala but in various countries throughout the world as well. Second, there has to be a much greater effort in trying to come to terms with these wrongs, especially by presenting and pressing the "why" question. To his credit, Clinton exercised a good deal of political leadership by even suggesting that U.S. foreign policy has not been what it should have been. But the effort has been halting and incomplete, and there has been no indication to date that the George W. Bush administration has any interest in carrying on with this reexamination of America's past. Finally, there also has to be a much greater attempt at transforming these wrongs. The biggest problem with transnational state apologies is that the apologizing state wants it both ways: it wants credit for recognizing and acknowledging a wrong against others, but it also wants the world to remain exactly as it had been before the apology was issued.

Yet, governments such as the United States that have committed wrongs grossly overstate what is demanded of them. Above all, victims seek acknowledgment of the manner in which powerful states have harmed them. They also want a promise that they will not become victims again. Finally, they want some assistance in overcoming the effects of these harmful actions.

APOLOGIES AND ETHICS

The apology phenomenon is best viewed as part of a much larger effort at seeking, establishing, and understanding the truth, exemplified in myriad truth commissions that have been created throughout the world. In a sense, the transnational state apology serves as a special kind of truth commission in the sense that it has become the vehicle for Western states to acknowledge their own involvement (or in the case of Rwanda, noninvolvement) in some of the world's horrors. But the comparison with truth commissions is instructive because it serves to underscore how hesitant and lacking so many state apologies have been. The U.S. apology to Guatemala is a case in point. Contrast Clinton's meager two-sentence apology with the voluminous report of an independent truth commission in Guatemala, which not only documented the atrocities committed by Guatemalan actors but also documented those involving the United States. The discrepancy, of course, is an enormous one. So is the fact that the apology itself pales next to the crime or the wrong that has been committed. However, there simply is no avoiding that. Still, this does not mean that we cannot apologize better than we have.

Apologies are ultimately about ethical standards, and they are as much about looking forward as they are about looking backward. An apology not only should seek to uncover wrongs from the past—that much should be fairly easy—but it should try to understand what it was about the ethical standards of that period that countenanced that kind of behavior. The answer, in most instances, is that people thought they were superior to other people, or else they have since come to understand the manner in which they used others for their own national ends and purposes. The ethics (or what passed itself off as such) at that time not only allowed this but often actually encouraged what we now consider inhumane behavior.[39]

Supposedly, we are well past this kind of nativist and racist thinking, and in many respects, we are. However what the stunning images from the Abu Ghraib prison in Iraq show quite clearly is that in many respects we are not. Yet, we continue to have great difficulty coming to terms with our actions and with ourselves. Thus, while President George W. Bush immediately expressed his "disgust" with these images, it took nearly a week before he issued an apology on behalf of the U.S. government and the American people, saying he was "sorry for the humiliation suffered by the Iraqi prisoners and the humiliation suffered by their families." Beyond the delayed response, the apology was negated at least in part by Bush's efforts at damage control when he went on to say that he was "equally sorry that people seeing these pictures didn't understand the true nature and heart of America."

The point is that these pictures *do* show a part—an important and undeniable part—of the "true nature and heart of America." What they show is what we explored in part I, namely, that our ethical and legal standards have allowed us to treat "others" as if they are inferior to "us." And until we begin to understand this, all of the apologies in the world (and to the world) will not change who we are and the manner in which we act in the world.

7

OUR BROTHERS' KEEPER

In fall 1997 an ethical uproar of sorts concerning the way in which Western drug manufacturers were testing AIDS medicines in Africa emerged.[1] The issue that was raised in the West at that time (interestingly enough, it was not so clear that the same ethical concerns existed outside of the West) involved whether giving placebos to a selected control group was unethical.[2] Those who attacked these practices argued that such testing would never be allowed in countries like the United States simply because medicine that might possibly extend a person's life was purposely being withheld, albeit for the advancement of science. After a short period of intense discussion, these companies decided to change their testing practices.[3] Either they came to recognize that testing in this manner violated certain ethical principles or else they simply sought to avoid the bad publicity engendered by the news coverage of this issue.

The question of whether there was an ethical duty to provide AIDS medicine to *all* of those who were infected with the disease (as opposed to providing it to all the participants in an AIDS drug test) was never raised as a part of the public discussion at that time. Thus, what apparently did not bother us very much was the enormous gap between the cost of AIDS medicine (between $10,000 and $15,000 per year) and the ability of people in the Third World to pay for this medicine. Instead, the ethical issue that was dealt with at that time—in fact, the only ethical issue involving AIDS in the Third World that those of us living in Western states were willing and able to deal with just a few short years ago—was whether a control group was a morally acceptable practice in AIDS drug testing. And in large part because of our own familiarity with the notion of "informed consent" and all that this has come to mean in the West, this method of testing was halted.

Of course, there had been discussion about the availability of AIDS medicine domestically. But what we could not conceive of in 1997 was extrapolating the ethical principles that were used in our domestic discussions of this issue to the larger world around us.[4] Somehow things were "different" out there. Or so we rationalized. The truth is that what we were really doing is what we do all the time, namely, selecting a small and discrete ethical issue—the manner of AIDS drug testing—and dealing with *that* issue. Thus, focusing on that issue then gave us license to ignore the larger and more important (but also more intractable) ethical issue of whether we have any kind of duty to assist *all* people who are infected with AIDS.

As you undoubtedly know, all of this has changed quite suddenly and quite dramatically, and there are now plans underway to make AIDS medicine widely available in Africa. What appears to have set all of this in motion was an offer by an Indian drug company to supply AIDS drugs at a price ($350 per year) that was just a fraction of what AIDS cocktails had cost previously.[5] What soon followed was a kind of political, economic, and ethical free-for-all. Generic drug manufacturers joined in the bidding to lower the costs of AIDS medicine, as did some of the giants of the pharmaceutical industry. Beyond this, drug manufacturers (eventually) decided to drop a lawsuit that had sought to prevent South Africa from importing cheaper anti-AIDS drugs and other medicines,[6] while the United Nations began a well-publicized effort to create a Global Health Fund of $7 billion to $10 billion primarily to fight AIDS.

Finally, what has been most noteworthy for purposes of our present discussion has been the change in policy (and ethics) of the United States. In 1999 the U.S. government allocated all of $200 million toward the Global Health Fund, an amount that borders on the symbolic, or worse. However, the level of financial commitment has steadily increased over time, and in his 2003 State of the Union address, Bush promised to increase U.S. spending on global AIDS to $15 billion over the next five years.

I cannot think of another ethical issue where the metamorphosis has been as complete and as rapid as this one has been. In the space of just a few short years, the issue of AIDS medicine in Third World countries has gone from being an ethical nonissue (at least for us), to a situation where the manner of testing (but only the manner of testing) raised certain kinds of ethical issues, to a situation where the assumption that Americans and other Westerners now seem to be working toward is one where it would be unethical *not* to provide AIDS medicine to all who are infected. Beyond that, there may well be additional ethical obligations to ensure that the health facilities in Third World countries that will handle the distribution of this AIDS medicine are up to certain standards.[7]

In his 2003 State of the Union address, Bush stated that "seldom has history offered a greater opportunity to do so much for so many."[8] The most remarkable thing is that we are starting to seize this opportunity.[9] In sum, what we appear to be living through is nothing less than a transformation of our entire ethical framework: millions of very sick people in distant lands who did not matter very much to us only a few short years ago now seem to matter a great deal.

IS IT ETHICS—OR IS IT SOMETHING ELSE?

There are at least three ways to respond to this claim: The first is to say that I am grossly overstating matters in the sense that if there is any kind of recognition of an ethical obligation, it is not one we feel ourselves,[10] but one we feel that pharmaceutical companies possess. In other words, making AIDS medicine affordable is not something we think that we as citizens of the richest country in the world have any obligation to do anything about (say by way of taxing ourselves and paying for this medicine through government revenue). But it is something we think that the drug companies ought to do, especially with the kinds of profits that they seem to be able to haul in each year.

There is, of course, a good deal of truth to this. It is always much easier to point to the ethical obligations that other people have than it is to recognize those that we possess ourselves. So perhaps to some extent we *are* pointing the finger of obligation at rich drug companies. However, referring back to our discussion of corporate behavior in chapter 1, when did we start to think of corporations as having ethical duties—especially to very poor and sick individuals in faraway lands?

The second retort is to say that the Western "response" has been (and continues to be) very inadequate. Such an argument has been made in an important article "International Obligation and HIV/AIDS," by Paul Harris and Patricia Siplon in the journal *Ethics and International Affairs*.[11] The position Harris and Siplon take is that Western states are not only guilty of nonfeasance because of the stingy amounts that they have given to fight AIDS in the Third World, but the authors take the position that the West is actually guilty of malfeasance because of the ways in which these countries have blocked measures that could relieve large-scale human suffering.

It is difficult to take issue with this argument as well, especially in light of the slight amount ($200 million) that the United States had pledged originally to the Global Health Fund. However, what has been somewhat more encouraging is that not only has the American commitment grown larger, but also the support for such measures has spread across the political spectrum.[12]

The third response is to say that the enormous drop in the price of AIDS medicine is not the result of any change in our ethical standards, but is simply a reflection of market realities. Given the fact that approximately two-thirds of the world's thirty-seven million people who are infected with AIDS live (and die) in sub-Saharan Africa and given the fact that it is a virtual certainty that only a very small percentage (between 1 percent and 2 percent of the infected population) are able to afford Western medicine,[13] by substantially lowering the price of AIDS medicine the drug manufacturers simply assured themselves of sales that they otherwise would not have made.

There is probably a good deal of truth to this argument as well, and I do not mean to discount this. However, my point is that, for whatever reason, our thinking has changed, and it has changed very dramatically. What has happened, I believe, is that we have started to make a connection between the devastation in Africa and ourselves—a connection, by the way, that had been made by most Africans a long time ago but which we are only now coming to understand. And not only have people in the West come to see how they could possibly help to extend the lives of tens of millions of people, but there also has been at least a tacit recognition that there is a moral obligation to do so.

But why AIDS? This is difficult to answer, but probably the reasons behind this new international effort and this new international vision are much the same as they have been in the domestic sphere. For one thing, this disease especially affects young people, and this certainly strikes a responsive chord. Added on to this is that the use of AIDS medicine during pregnancy sharply reduces the transmission of the disease from mother to child, and there are few things in life that are any crueler than to be born into the world with a fatal disease—especially one that is preventable. Thus, this does much to explain the concerted effort to halt the transmission of the disease in this manner. Beyond this, there are the physical manifestations of the disease. AIDS is often called the "thinness" disease in Africa, and the image of human beings wasting away to almost nothing is a very powerful and disturbing one indeed.

What also seems to be at work is some lingering guilt at the manner in which we have tended to view AIDS in the past. Recall that when the disease was first reported in the early 1980s, it was thought of as a "gay man's disease," and those who were infected by it were generally shunned. We now know that AIDS is not restricted to homosexuals (certainly Africa is proof of this), but there seems to be some effort to exorcise some of these prejudices from the past. In addition, for some period of time at least, Africans were "blamed" for AIDS, and this, too, seems to have played some part in how we have responded.

Finally, it must also be said that at least part of the reason behind the international effort that we are embarking on is the prospect of success.[14] Notwithstanding some racist comments by certain members of the Bush administration suggesting that Africans did not know the meaning of time and, thus, would not

be able to properly take AIDS medicine,[15] there is a general optimism that Western medicine will be able to substantially reduce
the levels of devastation in an already devastated continent.

As noteworthy as all this has been, perhaps the larger question is whether the international effort concerning AIDS in Africa
and in the rest of the Third World will fundamentally change
what we view as ethical behavior. To state matters bluntly, prior
to this time human suffering in other countries did not concern
us very much, and one reason it did not was that ignoring such
suffering was not viewed as an immoral action. Certainly there
were exceptions to our cavalier attitude, most notably (or at least
most visibly) the "We Are the World" moment in the mid-1980s
in response to starvation in Ethiopia. Yet, as soon as the novelty
wore off and the oft-played song grew old, our interest in becoming what we proclaimed we already were vanished almost immediately. The reason for this is that while our feelings toward
human suffering had changed (at least for a short while), what
had not changed was our ethical framework. And because of
this, in all good conscience we could walk away from the suffering of others when it suited our purposes to do so—and, invariably, it usually has served our purposes to do so.[16]

ARE WE THE WORLD—NOW?

But our ethical standards are changing—albeit in a slow, halting, and piecemeal fashion—and there have been other manifestations of this as well. One of the most noteworthy has been the
practice of humanitarian intervention.[17] Although this principle
of international law has existed for centuries, humanitarian
intervention has seldom been carried out—until very recently.[18]
Why were there so few interventions before, and why have there
been so many cases of humanitarian intervention within the
past decade?

The first part of this question is easier to answer. For one
thing, international law is premised on the notion of nonintervention. Article 2(4) of the United Nations Charter reads: "All
Members shall refrain in their international relations from the
threat or use of force against the territorial integrity or political

independence of any state" and Article 2(7) states: "Nothing contained in the present Charter shall authorize the United Nations to intervene in matters which are essentially within the domestic jurisdiction of any state." Under the UN Charter, states are only permitted to intervene when a situation inside another country threatens the peace and security of the international community and, then, only with the approval of the Security Council.[19]

However it is not simply international law that has prevented states from engaging in the practice of humanitarian intervention, but international politics as well. Most notably, political leaders almost universally subscribe to the idea that humanitarian intervention will be contrary to their own state's national interest—and it simply does not matter how desperate conditions are in other countries.[20]

Finally, and most importantly I think, until a very short time ago there simply was no moral imperative to intervene. In that way, then, the *legal* principle of nonintervention coincided with states' *political* interests in doing nothing, and these two were joined very nicely with an *ethical* framework that viewed human suffering elsewhere as somebody else's business—although it was never made clear whose business, exactly, it was.

As in the situation involving AIDS medicine, our ethical framework for intervention (and to a lesser extent the legal framework as well)[21] is now being stood on its head. Thus, rather than noninterference serving as the norm and intervention being the rarest of counterexamples, the premise we now seem to be heading toward is one in which humanitarian intervention is the norm (at least for certain areas of the globe), and it is noninterference that (somehow) will have to be justified.

This is not meant to suggest that the international community has intervened as much as it should or even that it has intervened well. In fact, many of our efforts have bordered on the cruel. Thus, although the intervention in Somalia was extraordinarily successful in that it prevented the starvation of some one hundred thousand people, American policymakers quickly abandoned Operation Restore Hope after eighteen U.S. Army Rangers were killed.[22] While Western states did engage in humanitarian intervention in Bosnia, they did so only after two hundred thousand Bosnian civilians had been killed and more than two million were displaced. And mention has already been made of the way in which Western states deliberately ignored the genocide in Rwanda in 1994. There was, of course, the French intervention in the form of Operation Turquoise, but it is difficult to think of an intervention that ended up providing a safe haven to those responsible for carrying out the genocide as being humanitarian.

These are some of the examples where Western states have intervened. In addition, there are a number of countries (i.e., Sierra Leone, the Democratic Republic of the Congo, Liberia, and Angola) where Western governments did not respond at all. To reiterate, I am not suggesting that humanitarian intervention is something that Western states have done well. However, what I *am* saying is that those of us living in Western societies now view human suffering in other lands differently than we had before.

The Jubilee 2000 debt forgiveness movement is another indication of this ethical change. That year, creditor states enacted a Heavily Indebted Poor Countries initiative that brought at least some debt relief to more than forty countries.[23] To give some indication of the levels of debt that we are talking about, the government in AIDS-ravaged Ghana will spend upwards of *twenty times* more money this year servicing its foreign debt than it will spend on fighting AIDS.

Of course, the Jubilee movement is not without its deficiencies. For one thing, only part of the debt will be forgiven. Another is that Western states and financial institutions are still very much in the business of making loans to the Third World, rather than outright grants, so there is a very good chance that this ugly cycle will only repeat itself. Finally, what Western states have purposefully ignored is the devastation that their trade barriers have brought to Third World people.[24] Apparently, it is much easier for us to write off loans—and appear magnanimous in doing so—than it is to change our protectionist trading practices. But unless all these things change, the stink of hypocrisy will overwhelm all of our humanitarian gestures.

Another striking development has been the newfound interest in enforcing human rights, although I hasten to point out that the American judiciary has been doing some of this for more than two decades (chapter 3). Without question, the most riveting case involved the international effort to extradite former Chilean dictator Augusto Pinochet (who was in England at the time) so that he could face criminal charges before a Spanish magistrate. Although the British government eventually allowed Pinochet to return to Chile based on purportedly humanitarian considerations, this case established an important principle under international law—the so-called Pinochet Principle—which is that those who direct or carry out human rights violations can (and hopefully will) be subject to prosecution wherever they may be found.[25]

Beyond Pinochet, international justice has been given a tremendous boost by the creation of the International Criminal Tribunal for Yugoslavia and the International Criminal Tribunal for Rwanda. Not only have both of these tribunals been responsible for the successful prosecution of a few war criminals, but perhaps more importantly, their existence has helped to pave the way for the creation of the International Criminal Court (ICC). Unfortunately, the U.S. government has been a vociferous opponent of the ICC, and the expressed fear is that American soldiers (as well as policymakers) could be subjected to trumped-up charges. This position is completely unfounded in that the Rome Statute creating the ICC specifies that it will defer to domestic prosecution as long as that state makes a "genuine" effort to prosecute a person who is alleged to have violated one of the four enumerated crimes.[26] However, this is completely consistent with what we saw in chapter 3, which is that the U.S. government maintains two sets of standards. One set of standards is for foreign nationals who commit human rights abuses. The second set of standards applies when the United States itself is accused of carrying out human rights violations.

Finally, if one looked hard enough, one would be able to see this new ethics of international responsibility behind (unfortunately, way behind) the recent surge in applying economic sanctions against other states. At their best, sanctions represent a clear moral condemnation of the human rights practices of other states—backed by economic and political power. In that way it can be said that individuals in one state are not deliberately ignoring the plight of "others." Unfortunately, economic sanctions have had a tendency to take on a life of their own, and they have been instituted (and removed) for virtually any kind of reason—but usually based on self-serving domestic considerations.[27] Much worse, however, Western sanctions have usually brought great harm to those they were purportedly intended to protect—and the best (meaning worst) evidence of this is the quarter of a million (or more) Iraqi children who died, at least partly as the result of Western sanctions.[28] The problem is that we have grown so enamored with our own humanitarianism that we have given ourselves license to act in just the opposite fashion. Perhaps economic sanctions should be eliminated altogether; better yet, sanctions should return to their humanitarian root, and they should only target the political and economic elite of an outlaw country rather than a general population that already has suffered enough.[29]

CONCLUSION

One of the questions that has long vexed humanity is the question Cain asked the Lord: Am I my brother's keeper? Although the question is as old as Genesis itself, until very recently the answer has been a negative one. Michael Ignatieff has commented on how suddenly this duty to others has arisen:

> It isn't obvious why strangers in peril halfway across the world *should* be our business. For most of human history, the boundaries of our moral universe were the borders of tribe, language, religion, or nation. The idea that we might have obligations to human beings beyond our borders simply because we belong to the same species is a recent invention, the result of our awakening to the shame of having done so little to help the millions of strangers who died in this century's experiments in terror and extermination.[30]

What we examined in this chapter are some examples of this awakening. Of these, the most remarkable has been the transformation of the AIDS epidemic in the Third World from something that was completely off our ethical radar screen just a few years ago to one where Western governments, Western drug companies, and Western people now act as if they have a duty to assist literally millions of desperately sick people. The larger question is where do we go from here? If we can now see the connection between Western medicine and the alleviation of human suffering with respect to AIDS, what other connections are we capable of making? Are we capable of understanding the connection between diseases other than AIDS and human suffering?[31] And are we able to understand the broader connection between poverty and human suffering—and the role that morality demands that we play?

CONCLUSION

It has been said repeatedly that the September 11, 2001, terrorist attacks on the World Trade Center and the Pentagon "will change everything—forever." The question I address in this final chapter is whether this tragedy has helped to make American society more ethical than it was before—or whether we have become less ethical people instead.

As I have explained in this book, American ethics and American ethical standards before September 11 were problematic at best. One thing that is certain is that the American people have a very deep interest in ethics. I think it is safe to say that there is no other country in which William Bennett's *The Book of Virtues* would be a best seller or a newspaper column like "The Ethicist" would be so popular. More than that, our schools teach values, our corporations address ethical concerns, our religions teach the "right" way, and moral issues are omnipresent in our popular culture. Without question, then, American society is permeated with "ethics."

Yet, despite all of this motion and noise, Americans have some strange ideas about ethics and what constitutes ethical behavior, and this is what we explored in part I. There is an expression that everybody wants to go to heaven but nobody wants to die. Much the same is true of our society's approach to ethics. We all want to be ethical people. Our problem—but, unfortunately, this really is also a problem for much of humankind as well—is that Americans have constructed a very limited and self-serving notion of what ethics is.

One manifestation of this is the premium placed on our own lives and the ethical issues we face daily, thereby imbuing many of life's most insignificant moments with more significance than they might otherwise deserve. At the same time, broader or more global ethical issues that truly do deserve enormous attention and resources are quietly but effectively placed to the side—until the point that they are ignored or else not treated as ethical issues.

Part I challenges this standard. The book's first five chapters provide examples of the hypocrisy and the inconsistency of some of our actions in the world. In particular, I argue that (1) U.S.-based multinational corporations have been regulated by U.S. law in a highly irregular (and unethical) manner; (2) the U.S. government has increasingly subjected foreign nationals to our laws without providing any form of constitutional protection; (3) U.S. courts are willing to pass judgment on the human rights practices of other states but not our own; (4) U.S. refugee policy is nowhere near as ethical as it holds itself out as being; and (5) American society is nowhere near as generous, as environmentally protective, or as "good" as it believes it is. What is even more insidious is that all of this has taken place amidst our great, national love affair with ethics and morality—a point that most assuredly has been noticed by the rest of the world.

Notwithstanding this less than stellar record, part II explores the manner in which we seem to be in the process of becoming more ethical people. The philosopher Henry Shue has a wonderfully succinct way of describing ethical obligations: "Why do we protect defenseless people? Because they are defenseless and they are people."[1] There are several ways in which we have protected defenseless people, but perhaps the most noteworthy has been the way in which we have started to recognize the humanity of AIDS victims and have begun to make Western medicine more widely available in the Third World.[2] Or as I stated earlier: very sick people in distant lands who had never been a part of our ethical framework before now seem to be.

But recognizing the humanity in "others" is just one part of this transformation. The American people also have shown at least some willingness of acknowledging their own inhumanity, best evidenced by the apologies that the United States has issued to people in several countries. Although I generally was critical of these efforts because they did not go nearly far enough in addressing our wrongs, it is important not to overlook their deeper meaning. For one thing, these apologies are as much about the present and the future as they are about our past, and they are a very strong indication that we do not want to be like those who came before us. These apologies are political statements but they are ethical statements as well. What they have said without equivocation is that our selfish obsession with our own "national interest" has sometimes brought great harm to other people. More than that, these apologies are our promise to be more ethical people in the future.

SEPTEMBER 11

This, then, takes us up to the events of September 11, and it is easy to see how our nation's suffering that day could take us back to our old version of ethics. Under this view, all that would matter (to us at least) is American suffering and American interests. Once again, we would come to view the world in terms of "us" versus "them"—essentially all of them. As before, we would set aside our legal and ethical standards when it served our purposes to do so—and, no doubt, it would often serve our purposes to do so. Along with that, we would apply one set of standards for ourselves and a completely different set of standards (perhaps no standards at all) in our dealings with others. Of course, we would continue to be "ethical"—or at least posture as such. However, as in the past, our ethics (or what we would attempt to pass off as such) would be used to promote and protect our country's "national interest"—but essentially nothing more than that. The truth is that our ethics would be the antithesis of true ethics. Rather than "integrating the existence and the fate of others into our vision of ourselves" we would do just the opposite.[3]

Unfortunately, there are a number of indications that this is exactly where we are heading. One of the most disturbing manifestations of this has been the secret detention of between fifteen hundred and two thousand Muslim men on the grounds that they were "suspected terrorists," although not a single person arrested in this national dragnet has been charged with any involvement in the September 11 attacks.

Under our old ethics and our old law, the U.S. Constitution did not travel outside the country unless the interests of an American citizen were involved or unless a foreign national had developed "substantial connections" with this country (whatever that means). The war on terrorism not only has underscored this dichotomy, but in many respects, has been built on it. In that way, the government purposely selected a detention site outside the country's territorial jurisdiction (Guantanamo Bay, Cuba) as a means of denying al Qaeda operatives (or, more accurately, those suspected as such) any constitutional protection.

Some of the implications of this have already manifested themselves. For one thing, the George W. Bush administration has announced that only a handful of captives would be tried and that it would not be under any obligation to free those acquitted in a court of law.[4] More ominously, perhaps, has been the treatment of suspected terrorists in other lands. Addressing the status of the war on terrorism in his 2003 State of the Union address, Bush stated: "All told, more than 3,000 suspected terrorists have been arrested in many countries. And many others have met a different fate. They are no longer a problem for the United States and our friends and allies."[5] The implication of this, of course, is that these suspects have been summarily executed.

Yet, in many respects the war on terrorism threatens to take us in the opposite direction and to collapse the distinction between home and abroad in the sense that constitutional protection within the United States is starting to look dangerously like constitutional protection outside the country. The most disturbing manifestation of this is the position of the executive branch that it alone will determine who qualifies as an "enemy combatant" and the conditions under which those so accused are held. And note that this includes not only foreign nationals but American citizens as well.

In this book I have talked about an "old" ethics and a "new" ethics. However, one reason why it is so difficult to differentiate between these two is that we have always postured as ethical people and readily employed the language of morality—even when our actions were anything but this. In that vein, then, consider American foreign aid in the post–September 11 period. In his 2002 State of the Union address Bush made repeated references to the great values of this country and the enormous compassion of the American people. The following is a sampling of these remarks:

> America needs citizens to extend the compassion of our country to every part of the world. . . . This time of adversity offers a unique moment of opportunity, a moment we must seize to change our culture. Through the gathering momentum of millions of acts of service and decency and kindness, I know we can overcome evil with greater good.
>
> [Continuing] And we have a great opportunity during this time of war to lead the world toward the values that will bring lasting peace. All fathers and mothers, in all societies, want their children to be educated and live free from poverty and violence. No people on earth yearn to be oppressed or aspire to servitude or eagerly await the midnight knock of the secret police.
>
> [And finally] America will lead by defending liberty and justice because they are right and true and unchanging for all people everywhere.[6]

These are stirring words. However, the problem is that our actions belie our words. Just one day before this address, Bush had summarily rejected an international proposal initiated by UN Secretary General Kofi Annan and Gordon Brown, Britain's chancellor of the exchequer, whereby rich, industrialized states would double their foreign aid in the wake of the war in Afghanistan.[7] Recall that the United States is the *least* generous country in the world—despite what the American people might think. To me, this episode epitomizes so much of American ethics. Talk a good game but do not do anything to back up this talk. Describe endlessly how good and how moral and how compassionate this country is. But then reject out of hand a plan where we might actually act in that fashion. Talk and talk and talk about creating a new world order, but arm ourselves to the teeth and ignore the human suffering that helps to give rise to such things as terrorism. Constantly invoke the imagery of worldwide cooperation and goodwill, but systematically ignore those who would take issue with American policy. Use international law to condemn the practices of others, but repeatedly and conveniently ignore this same law when it is viewed as being inimical to American interests.[8] This, in short, is our ethics of old, and I have a very deep fear that we are in the process of reverting back to this.

There is, however, another path that September 11 could take us on. It is a path that decidedly rejects this ethics of the past, and it is actually the ethics that we were in the process of developing before that fateful day. If nothing else, the attacks on September 11 should show us that we are all, in some way at least, defenseless people, to use Shue's terminology. Moreover, our own country's suffering could (and should) give us a much greater understanding and empathy for the suffering of so much of humankind. September 11 will forever be a day of national tragedy, and rightly so. However, there is no reason why it cannot also be honored for the courage and compassion displayed by so many Americans that day and in the immediate aftermath. In short, while September 11 has exacerbated some of the worst tendencies in American life, it also has brought forth some of our country's finest qualities.

My wish is to end this on a positive note, and I will point to two such developments. One is that in a meeting on addressing world poverty held in Monterrey, Mexico, in spring 2002, the West's Holy Grail itself—globalization—was publicly questioned by policymakers in industrialized states for the very first time.[9] Given the fact that the levels of inequality between the West and the rest of the world have been widening for decades, this public pronouncement could have been made a long time ago. However, the more important point is that we have come to publicly acknowledge that the world cannot continue to exist in two separate and distinct spheres, and the solution that Western countries have been pushing simply has not worked as we have promised. The problem, once again, is that recognizing our immoral actions is one thing and that constructing meaningful policies to address these wrongs is something else altogether different.

The second example takes us back to the issue of American foreign aid. Two months after rejecting the Annan–Brown proposal to double foreign aid, Bush agreed to increase the United States foreign aid budget from $10 billion a year (which is the same amount that it had been for a decade) to $15 billion over the course of a three-year period. These amounts, of course, are nowhere near the levels that a moral nation would provide—but it is a start. Perhaps what is even more noteworthy is the connection made between poverty and terrorist activities. In remarks accompanying this announcement Bush stated that "persistent poverty and oppression can lead to hopelessness and despair. And when governments fail to meet the most basic needs of their people, these failed states can become havens for terror."[10]

Terrorism aside, we have to learn a much deeper lesson. What we have to understand is the manner in which we have shown a terrible tendency to ignore the humanity of other people. And in doing this, what we also have done is to deny the humanity in ourselves.

NOTES

NOTES TO INTRODUCTION

1. Certainly, many of the worst human rights abuses in history have been carried out under the aegis of religion. In his wonderful piece of scholarship dealing with the Western genocide of various indigenous peoples, Mark Cocker shows the way in which religion was employed to justify the killing and displacement of literally hundreds of millions. Mark Cocker, *Rivers of Blood, Rivers of Gold: Europe's Conquest of Indigenous Peoples* (New York: Grove Press, 1998).

2. Although "morality" and "ethics" have the same roots, a theoretical distinction between the two should be noted. Mark Amstutz explains this difference: "Strictly speaking . . . the two terms represent distinct elements of normative analysis: *morality* referring to values and beliefs about what is right and wrong, good and bad, just and unjust and *ethics* referring to the examination, justification, and critical analysis of morality." Mark R. Amstutz, *International Ethics: Concepts, Theories, and Cases in Global Politics* (Lanham, MD: Rowman & Littlefield, 1999), 3. Although I recognize this distinction, my own preference is to employ common usage and conflate the two.

3. This phenomenon is by no means restricted to the public and even seems to afflict those who do this as a profession. In his insightful book *American Heat*, Donald Brown argues that environmental ethicists have largely ignored the issue of global warming, and the reason why they have done so is that they have focused on a battery of less pressing environment-related issues. In the book's preface he writes:

> Many environmental ethicists are focused on issues that are not connected to crucial and pressing environmental ethical ques-

tions. That is, the focus of many environmental ethicists and theologians has been directed largely at such metaethical questions as whether humans have duties to animals and plants and what is the nature and source of a religious environmental ethic. Although these are important questions and are very relevant to some practical issues, as this book demonstrates, they have little to do with many of the environmental controversies that are unfolding right in front of us at this moment in history. For this reason, extraordinarily important ethical issues are being overlooked by many of our most concerned philosophers and theologians.

Donald A. Brown, *American Heat: Ethical Problems with the United States' Response to Global Warming* (Lanham, MD: Rowman & Littlefield, 2002), xviii.

4. Different authors use different terminology. For example, Larry May and Shari Collins-Sharratt refer to this as a distinction between "personal" and "social" ethics. *Applied Ethics: A Multicultural Approach* (New York: Prentice Hall, 1999), 4. Whatever you term it, my point remains the same: our society has come to place a premium on "personal" ethics at the expense of "social" ethics.

5. Randy Cohen, "The Ethicist," *New York Times Magazine*, April 15, 2001, 15–16.

6. To be fair, in a book that is based on these columns, Cohen shows a much greater appreciation of the relationship between micro- and macrolevel ethics. At one point in an introductory essay in the book he writes: "Just as individual ethics can only be understood in relation to the society within which it is practiced, it is also true that individual ethical behavior is far likelier to flourish within a just society. Indeed, it might be argued that to lead an ethical life one must work to build a just society." Randy Cohen, *The Good, the Bad & the Difference: How to Tell Right from Wrong in Everyday Situations* (New York: Doubleday, 2002), 9

7. Of course, Boeing is not the only corporation that teaches "ethics" to its employees. Rather, nearly all corporations do including the now-disgraced Enron Corporation whose "Code of Ethics" was reportedly being sold on e-Bay for $100. The point is that ethics is not always a good thing. At the same time that the employees of corporations are being subjected to all sorts of ethical codes and challenges, top management might be making off with the company's pension fund. Or as in the case of Boeing, top management may be stealing documents from its rivals and defrauding the U.S. government. Leslie Wayne,

"Chief Executive at Boeing Quits under Criticism," *New York Times*, December 2, 2003, A1.

8. Paul Krugman, "For Richer: How the Permissive Capitalism of the Boom Destroyed American Equality," *New York Times Magazine*, October 20, 2002, 64.

9. Michael Walzer discusses this problem in an article entitled "The Big Shrug." After citing a series of statistics on growing inequality in the United States, Walzer writes:

No one seems to care about any of this. I suppose that's an exaggeration. The people who organize the studies obviously care, and they are trying to get others to care. But their general strategy—issuing reports in tones of surprised discovery and barely repressed outrage—doesn't seem to be working.

Michael Walzer, "The Big Shrug," *New Republic*, February 2, 1998.

10. Section 502B of the Foreign Assistance Act, 22 U.S. Code § 2304, reads: "Except under circumstances specified in this Section, no security assistance may be provided to any country the government of which engages in a consistent pattern of gross violations of internationally recognized human rights."

Notwithstanding this language, there is an escape clause whereby assistance may still be provided if the president certifies that "extraordinary circumstances" exist warranting the provision of such assistance.

11. See, for example, Dawn Miller, "Security at What Cost? Arms Transfers to the Developing World and Human Rights," in *Understanding Human Rights: New Systematic Studies*, ed. Sabine Carey and Steven C. Poe (Hampshire, UK: Ashgate Publishing, forthcoming); Clair Apodaca and Michael Stohl, "United States Human Rights Policy and Foreign Assistance," *International Studies Quarterly* 43 (1999): 185–98. Mark Hertsgaard estimates that 90 percent of U.S. arms sales go to undemocratic or human rights–abusing governments. Mark Hertsgaard, *The Eagle's Shadow: Why America Fascinates and Infuriates the World* (New York: Picador, 2002), 83.

12. Andrew J. Pierre, ed. *Cascade of Arms: Managing Conventional Weapons Proliferation* (Washington, DC: Brookings Institute, 1997), 5.

13. Michael Ignatieff uses this very example in a discussion of why "human rights" has come to be rejected by so much of the non-Western countries. He writes:

If taken seriously, human rights values put interests into question, interests such as sustaining a larger export sector in a nation's defense industry, for example. It becomes incoherent for states like Britain and the United States to condemn Indonesia or Turkey for their human rights performance while providing their military with vehicles or weapons that can be used for the repression of civilian dissent. When values do not actually constrain interests, an "ethical foreign policy"—the self-proclaimed goal of Britain's Labour government—becomes a contradiction in terms.

Michael Ignatieff, *Human Rights as Politics and Idolatry* (Princeton, NJ: Princeton University Press, 2001), 22–23.

14. In the year 2000, arms sales rose for the third straight year to $36.9 billion. Thom Shanker, "Global Arms Sales Rise Again, and the U.S. Heads the Pack," *New York Times*, August 20, 2001, A3. However, in the year 2001 arms sales were reduced considerably, falling to their lowest level since 1997. Thom Shanker, "Global Arms Sales to Developing Nations Are Tumbling, Study Finds," *New York Times*, August 8, 2002, A8.

15. In addressing how and why it is that massive levels of world poverty continue to exist in the world, Thomas Pogge makes the argument that this ethical issue is simply not viewed as an "ethical issue": "Extensive, severe poverty can continue, because we do not find its eradication morally compelling. And we cannot find its eradication morally compelling until we find its persistence and the relentless rise in global inequality troubling enough to warrant serious moral reflection." Thomas Pogge, *World Poverty and Human Rights: Cosmopolitan Responsibilities and Reforms* (Malden, MA: Polity, 2002), 3.

16. V. Rock Grundman, "The New Imperialism: The Extraterritorial Application of United States Law," *International Lawyer* 14 (1980): 257–66.

17. For an excellent presentation of this argument see Elazar Barkan, *The Guilt of Nations: Restitution and Negotiating Historical Injustices* (New York: Norton, 2000).

18. Jonathan Glover, *Humanity: A Moral History of the Twentieth Century* (New Haven, CT: Yale University Press, 1999), 6.

19. Rather than relying on preexisting principles, Elazar Barkan argues that "restitution" is itself a theory of international relations, although it proposes a process and not a specific solution or standard. See Barkan, *The Guilt of Nations*.

20. Daniel Jonah Goldhagen, *A Moral Reckoning: The Role of the Catholic Church in the Holocaust and Its Unfulfilled Duty of Repair* (New York: Knopf, 2002).

21. Goldhagen, *A Moral Reckoning*, 123.

22. Jean-Marc Coicaud and Daniel Warner, "Reflections on the Extent and Limits of Contemporary Ethics," in *Ethics and International Affairs: Extent and Limits*, edited by Jean-Marc Coicaud and Daniel Warner (New York: United Nations University, 2001), 1–2.

NOTES TO CHAPTER 1

1. Diana B. Henriques, "Black Mark for a 'Good Citizen,'" *New York Times*, November 26, 1995, sec. 3, A1.

2. Henriques, "Black Mark for a 'Good Citizen,'" sec. 3, A1.

3. Calvin Sims, "In Peru, a Fight for Fresh Air," *New York Times*, December 12, 1995, C1.

4. Diana Jean Schemo, "Pesticide from U.S. Kills the Hopes of Fruit Pickers in the Third World," *New York Times*, December 6, 1995, A12.

5. An interesting variation on this theme involves energy plants that are being built just over the California border in Mexico. Although nearly all the energy that will be produced will be used in the United States, these plants will be "governed" by Mexico's very weak environmental standards. Tim Weiner, "U.S. Will Get Power, and Pollution, from Mexico," *New York Times*, September 17, 2002, A3.

6. 213 U.S. 347 (1909).

7. The facts of the case are noteworthy enough to mention. An American businessperson named McConnell purchased a banana plantation in Panama, which at that time was still a part of Colombia. United Fruit Company, a U.S. corporation aggressively seeking to monopolize the Central American banana trade, promptly contacted McConnell. In Godfather-like fashion, United Fruit provided McConnell with two choices: either sell the plantation to them or get out of the business. McConnell refused both "offers," but later sold his plantation to the American Banana Company, a newly established enterprise run out of Alabama.

After this, Costa Rica invaded the then-independent Panama, allegedly at United Fruit's bequest. Costa Rican forces seized American Banana's plantation and gave it to a person named Atsua, who immediately sold it to United Fruit. Having lost its plantation, American Banana shifted venues from the battlefield to the courtroom and brought an antitrust action against United Fruit. American Banana charged United Fruit with the following anticompetitive acts: conspiring with other banana producers, interfering with American Banana's contracts, and below-cost bidding.

8. 213 U.S. at 355.

9. *Id.* at 356.

10. United States v. Pacific & Arctic Co., 228 U.S. 87 (1913); Thomsen v. Cayser, 243 U.S. 66 (1917); United States v. Sisal Sales Corp., 274 U.S. 268 (1927); United States v. Aluminum Co. of Am., 148 F. 2d 416 (2d Cir. 1945); Timberlane Lumber Co. v. Bank of Am., 549 F. 2d 597 (9th Cir. 1977).

11. Steele v. Bulova, 344 U.S. 280 (1952).

12. Bersch v. Drexel Firestone, Inc., 519 F. 2d 974 (2d Cir. 1975)

13. 499 U.S. 244 (1991).

14. Civil Rights Acts of 1964, Pub. L. No. 88–352, Title VII, 78 Stat. 253 (codified as amended 42 U.S.C. §§ 2000a–2000h-6). The act states that it is an unlawful employment practice: (1) to fail or refuse to hire or to discharge any individual, or otherwise to discriminate against any individual with respect to his compensation, terms, conditions, or privileges of employment, because of such individual's race, color, religion, sex, or national origin; or (2) to limit, segregate, or classify employees or applicants for employment in any way that would deprive or tend to deprive any individual of employment opportunities or otherwise adversely affect his status as an employee, because of such individual's race, color, religion, sex, or national origin.

15. 499 U.S. at 248.

16. *Id.*

17. *Id.*

18. Boureslan based his argument that the act applied extraterritorially on three separate grounds: The first is that Title VII prohibits discriminatory acts by employers engaged in "commerce" that is defined as any activity involving "trade, traffic, commerce, transportation, or communication among the several States, or between a State and any place outside thereof." Because the definition of "state" already included the territory of the United States, it was argued that "any place outside thereof" must refer to foreign commerce. The second argument was based on Title VII's so-called alien exemption which provides that the statute "shall not apply to an employer with respect to the employment of aliens outside any State." Boureslan argued that there would be no need to exempt aliens abroad unless the statute had an extraterritorial application. Finally, it was argued that the Court should defer to EEOC guidelines that for some time had interpreted Title VII to protect Americans employed abroad.

19. The Civil Rights Act of 1991, Pub. L. No. 102–66, § 109 (c), 105

Stat. 1071 (1991) (codified at scattered sections of 42 U.S.C.). There was precedent in this response. In 1984 Congress amended the Age Discrimination in Employment Act (ADEA) to apply extraterritorially after several lower courts had restricted the act to a territorial application.

20. Of course, the readily understood meaning of "American corporation" seems to be in the process of changing as a number of U.S.-based corporations have "moved" outside the United States in order to avoid U.S. taxes. Perhaps the best-known case involves Stanley Works, the maker of black-and-yellow tools, which has operated out of its headquarters in New Britain, Connecticut, for 159 years but now has plans to "move" to Bermuda—but only for tax purposes. Editorial, "The Bermuda Tax Triangle," *New York Times*, May 13, 2002, A18.

21. Congressional intent is clearest in statutes that specify one way or the other whether a statute is to have an extraterritorial application. For example, § 175 of the Biological Weapons Anti-Terrorism Act states: "There is extraterritorial federal jurisdiction over an offense under this section committed by or against a national of the United States." Similarly, the Maritime Drug Law Enforcement Act explicitly spells out the act's extraterritorial scope. In a section entitled "Extension beyond the territorial jurisdiction of the United States," there is language to the effect that "this section is intended to reach acts of possession, manufacture, or distribution committed outside the territorial jurisdiction of the United States." 46 U.S.C. app. § 1903 (h) (1988). On the other hand, one of the clearest examples where Congress has given an unequivocal territorial limitation to a statute is the Fair Labor Standards Act, which specifically excludes certain sections from applying to employees in a workplace "within a foreign country." 29 U.S.C. § 213 (1988).

The problem is that most statutes give no indication one way or the other, thus leaving the judiciary in the position of having either to guess or to "make" law itself. More problematic still are those statutes that seem to indicate an extraterritorial intent but which the judiciary has given a territorial reading. For example, one of the leading cases in this area is *Foley Bros., Inc. v. Filardo*, 336 U.S. 281 (1949). In that case, a U.S. citizen working on U.S. government public works projects in Iran and Iraq brought suit claiming protections under the Eight Hour Law. The statute applies to "every contract made to which the United States" is a party. Notwithstanding this language, however, the Supreme Court gave the act a territorial reading, and the plaintiff was not able to receive any of the protections provided by the Eight Hour Law.

Perhaps the environmental case law provides us with the most puzzling and troublesome results, and much of this has revolved around
the National Environmental Policy Act of 1969 (NEPA), 42 U.S.C. §§
4321–79 (1982). NEPA mandates that federal agencies must issue environmental impact statements (EIS) for projects undertaken by the federal government. Although the statute is replete with seemingly
extraterritorial language "recognizing the . . . critical importance of
restoring and maintaining environmental quality to the overall welfare
and development of man," the statute has been restricted to having a
territorial scope. Amlon Metals, Inc. v. FMC Corp. 775 F. Supp. 668
(S.D.N.Y. 1991); Greenpeace v. Stone, 748 F. Supp. 749 (D. Haw. 1990);
Natural Resources Defense Council v. N.R.C., 647 F. 2d 1345 (D.C. Cir.
1981).

22. Mark Gibney and R. David Emerick, "The Extraterritorial Applica-
tion of United States Law and the Protection of Human Rights: Holding
Multinational Corporations to Domestic and International Standards,"
Temple International and Comparative Law Journal 10 (1996): 123–45.

23. Mark Gibney, "The Extraterritorial Application of U.S. Law: The
Perversion of Democratic Governance, the Reversal of Institutional
Roles, and the Imperative of Establishing Normative Principles," *Boston
College International and Comparative Law Review* 19 (1996): 297–321.

24. I single out these areas of law for two reasons: The first is that
while such things as minimum wage or the number of hours that
employees can work would (and should) differ from country to country,
what does not change (and should not change) is the need for a safe
and healthy workplace and a clean environment. In addition, most
Third World states have not legislated extensively in these areas. Thus,
there is more of a need to offer protection at the same time that there is
less of a possibility of a "conflict" arising between the extraterritorial
application of U.S. law and the law of the foreign state.

25. There is precedent for this. In response to much of the criticism
that has been directed at its overseas practices, the Nike corporation
has announced that it would abide by U.S. safety and environmental
laws in all of its overseas operations. John H. Cushman Jr., "Nike
Pledges to End Child Labor and Apply U.S. Rules Abroad," *New York
Times*, May 13, 1998, D1.

26. Another "moral" issue that previously had been addressed by
U.S. law was antiapartheid measures for U.S.-based corporations
doing business in South Africa while it was under white-minority rule.
Under the terms of the Comprehensive Anti-Apartheid Act of 1986, 22
U.S.C. §§ 5001–116, American corporations employing more than

twenty-five people in South Africa were required to comply with a Code of Conduct adopted along the lines of the Sullivan Principles.

27. Foreign Corrupt Practices Act of 1977, Pub. L. No. 95–213, 91 Stat. 1494 (1977) (codified at 15 U.S.C. § 78dd-1).

28. A weak alternative to applying U.S. environmental law extraterritorially is a proposal before the U.S. Congress to institute an international "right to know" that would require large corporations that are traded on U.S. stock exchanges and have significant international operations to disclose certain information to affected communities. A *New York Times* editorial endorsed the measure but in a rather backhanded fashion.

> The idea of an international right to know is a creative and, for the companies, a not particularly burdensome new approach. American companies could still behave badly if they chose to do so. The law does not prevent irresponsible mining companies in Peru from spilling mercury on local roads, or toy makers in China from employing children. But they would have to tell the public about these practices, and let the market, and public opinion, go to work.

Editorial, "An International Right to Know," *New York Times*, January 25, 2003, A34.

29. Perhaps the most extreme and unsettling case in which U.S. safety law was not given an extraterritorial reading involved the sale of a Westinghouse Corporation nuclear power reactor to the Philippines. According to the plan of the Filipino government, the plant was to be situated above an earthquake fault line and below an active volcano. In addition to these logistical considerations (nightmares?), the technical design of the plant did not meet domestic (U.S.) standards. Despite these grave flaws, the U.S. Nuclear Regulatory Commission voted to issue the plant's license on the grounds that it did not have the jurisdiction under U.S. law to consider the safety and environmental effects on the citizens of a recipient state or even to consider the effects of an exported reactor on U.S. interests and U.S. citizens abroad (including American soldiers based in the Philippines). This decision was upheld on appeal. Natural Res. Def. Council, Inc. v. Nuclear Regulatory Commission, 647 F. 2d 1345 (D.C. Cir. 1981). For an excellent account and critique of this case see Anthony D'Amato and Kirsten Engel, "State Responsibility for the Exportation of Nuclear Power Technology," *Virginia Law Review* 74 (1988): 1011–66. Luckily for all of us, the Filipino government decided not to proceed with the project.

30. 330 U.S. 501 (1947).

31. *Id.* at 508.

32. 454 U.S. 235 (1981).

33. *See, e.g.,* Sibaja v. Dow Chem. Co., 757 F. 2d 1215 (11th Cir., 1985); Delgado v. Shell Oil Co., 890 F. Supp.1324 (S.D. Tex. 1995); Sequihua v. Texaco, 847 F. Supp. 61 (1994); Cabalceta v. Standard Fruit Co., 667 F. Supp. 833 (S.D. Fla. 1987) *aff'd in part and rev'd in part* 883 F. 2d 1553 (11th Cir. 1989); In re Union Carbide Corp. Gas Plant Disaster, 634 F. Supp. 842 (S.D.N.Y. 1986); *aff'd in part and rev'd in part,* 809 F. 2d 195 (2d Cir. 1987). David Robertson, a professor of law at the University of Texas, conducted an informal study showing that of fifty-five personal injury cases filed by foreign plaintiffs in the United States and dismissed on the basis of *forum non conveniens,* ten were tried elsewhere and twenty were settled. Of the twenty settled, sixteen settled for less than half of the asserted value of their claims. David Robertson, "Forum Non Conveniens in America and England," *Law Quarterly Review* 103 (1987): 398–432.

34. 886 S.W. 2d 674 (Tex. 1990).

35. *Id.* at 681.

36. David Gonzalez and Samuel Loewenberg, "Banana Workers Get Day in Court," *New York Times,* January 18, 2003, B1.

37. Juan Forero, "Texaco Goes on Trial in Ecuador Pollution Case," *New York Times,* October 23, 2003, W1.

38. Gonzalez and Loewenberg, "Banana Workers Get Day," W1.

39. Flores et al. v. S. Peru Copper Corp., Lexsee 2002 U.S. Dist. Lexis 13013 (2002), *aff'd,* 343 F. 3d 140 (2d Cir. 2003).

NOTES TO CHAPTER 2

1. Ethan Nadelmann describes the veritable explosion in the extraterritorial application and enforcement of U.S. criminal statutes this way.

As recently as the early 1980s most crimes committed overseas that did not directly affect United States security or territorial interests were not subject to United States jurisdiction. Today, a terrorist who harms an American citizen anywhere in the world has violated not just the law of the *situs* but United States law as well. Moreover, the longstanding reluctance of law enforcement officials to pursue their investigations overseas has faded considerably. Issues of extraterritoriality now dominate discussions of international law enforcement more than ever before.

Ethan Nadelmann, "The Role of the United States in the International Enforcement of Criminal Law," *Harvard International Law Journal* 31 (1990): 37–76, 39.

2. See generally, Mark Gibney, "Policing the World: The Long Reach of U.S. Law and the Short Arm of the Constitution," *Connecticut Journal of International Law* 6 (1990): 103–26.

3. 494 U.S. 259 (1990).

4. *Id.* at 266.

5. *Id.* at 272.

6. *Id.* at 273.

7. *Id.* at 285.

8. *Id.* at 275 (citations omitted).

9. *Id.* at 278.

10. *Id.*

11. Realistically, having the search conducted by foreign officers is one means of avoiding this scenario—operating in tandem with American officials (of course).

12. 494 U.S. at 283–84.

13. *Id.* at 288 (emphasis in original).

14. *Id.* at 292.

15. The Fifth Amendment reads as follows:

> No person shall be held to answer for a capital, or otherwise infamous crime, unless on a presentment or indictment of a Grand Jury, except in cases arising in the land or naval forces, or in the Militia, when in actual service in time of War or public danger; nor shall any person be subject for the same offence to be twice put in jeopardy of life or limb, nor shall be compelled in any criminal case to be a witness against himself, nor be deprived of life, liberty or property, without due process of law; nor shall private property be taken for public use, without just compensation.

16. 494 U.S. at 264 (citations omitted).

17. The Supreme Court recently reaffirmed this holding in *Chavez v. Martinez*, 538 U.S. 760 (2003). In this case a police officer questioned a suspect off and on for forty-five minutes while he was lying on a stretcher having just been shot in the face at close range by one officer and in the back and knees by a second officer. Martinez, who was blinded and paralyzed by his wounds, repeatedly cried out in pain and begged for treatment and said that he did not want to talk. Relying on its decision in *Verdugo-Urquidez*, the Court held that no constitutional rights were violated because the information obtained from the defendant was not used against him in a criminal trial.

18. 494 U.S. at 269.

19. 339 U.S. 763 (1950).

20. 745 F. 2d 1500 (D.C. Cir. 1984) (en banc) *vacated and rem'd*, 471 U.S. 1113 (1985) (remanded in light of the Foreign Assistance and Related Appropriations Act, 1985, and efforts by Honduras to make restitution), *rev'd*, 788 F. 2d 762 (D.C. Cir. 1986) (withdrawal of U.S. personnel fundamentally altered the balance of equities).

21. 745 F. 2d at 1513.

22. *Id.* at 1512.

23. *Id.* at 1515.

24. *Id.* at 1515–16.

25. *Id.* at 1516–17.

26. Harbury v. Deutch, 233 F. 3d 596 (D.C. Cir. 2000).

27. In spring 2002 the Supreme Court held that Harbury's "access to courts" claim was insufficient, and it remanded the case back to the lower courts. Christopher v. Harbury, 536 U.S. 403 (2002).

28. 504 U.S. 655 (1992).

29. United States v. Caro-Quintero, 745 F. Supp. 599, 602–4, 609 (C.D. Cal. 1990).

30. Extradition Treaty, May 4, 1978, 1979. United States–United Mexican States, 31 U.S.T. 5059, T.I.A.S. No. 9656.

31. Caro-Quintero, 745 F. Supp. at 614.

32. United States v. Verdugo-Urquidez, 939 F. 2d 1341, 1350 (9th Cir. 1991).

33. 119 U.S. 436 (1886).

34. *Id.* at 444.

35. 500 F. 2d 267 (2d Cir. 1974).

36. *Id.* at 275.

37. 510 F. 2d 62, 65 (2d Cir. 1975).

38. Seth Mydans, "Judge Clears Mexican in Agent's Killing," *New York Times*, December 15, 1992, A20.

39. For an excellent treatment of the *Alvarez-Machain* case and of the law of extradition in general, see Christopher H. Pyle, *Extradition, Politics, and Human Rights* (Philadelphia, PA: Temple University Press, 2001).

40. Alvarez-Machain v. United States, D.C. No. CV-93–04072-SVW-06 (9th Cir. 2003).

41. In fact, the executive branch has gone so far as to say that the judiciary should play no role in the government's war on terrorism. However, this issue at least has been put to rest after the Supreme Court granted certiorari to hear cases involving the Guantanamo Bay detainees.

42. Eyal Press, "In Torture We Trust?" *Nation*, March 31, 2003.
43. Act of October 26, 2001, Pub. L. 107–56, 115 Stat. 272.
44. Adam Liptak, Neil A. Lewis, and Benjamin Weiser, "After Sept. 11, a Legal Battle on the Limits of Civil Liberty," *New York Times*, August 4, 2002, A1; Hamdi v. Rumsfeld, 316 F. 3d 450 (4th Cir. 2003).
45. David Cole, "Patriot Act's Big Brother," *Nation*, March 17, 2003.

NOTES TO CHAPTER 3

1. 976 F. 2d 1328 (9th Cir. 1992).
2. 630 F. 2d 876 (2d Cir. 1980).
3. 28 U.S.C. § 1350.
4. 630 F. 2d at 884.
5. The leading case going against the long line of *Filartiga* cases is *Tel-Oren v. Libyan Arab Republic*, 517 F. Supp. 542 (D.D.C. 1981) *aff'd*, 726 F. 2d 774 (D.C. Cir. 1984). *Tel-Oren* revolved around a 1978 terrorist incident in Israel. Thirteen members of the Palestinian Liberation Organization (PLO) landed a boat in Israel and hijacked a bus. In a confrontation with Israeli security, the members of the PLO shot at their hostages and blew up the bus, killing thirty-four adults and children and wounding seventy-five others. Survivors of the attack sued in federal district court in the District of Columbia, basing jurisdiction on the ATS. The plaintiffs included Israeli, Dutch, and American citizens.

Affirming the district court's dismissal of the case, the panel for the D.C. Circuit deciding the case on the merits issued a one-page *per curiam* opinion, accompanied by lengthy concurring opinions from each of the three judges. Judge Edwards' opinion came the closest to the reasoning of the court in *Filartiga*. Edwards was of the opinion that the ATS did provide a cause of action for aliens asserting violations of the law of nations. However, Edwards based dismissal on the fact that while the law of nations prohibits torture by state actors and people acting under color of state law, the PLO was not subject to the same standards of international law.

Judge Bork's order for dismissal was based on a number of factors. One was that such a suit would violate separation of powers principles. Bork also took the position that while the ATS granted jurisdiction, it did not also create a cause of action for the individual alien. Finally, Bork would restrict violations of the law of nations to those recognized in 1789 when the ATS was enacted as federal law: violation of safe-conduct, infringement on ambassadorial rights, and piracy.

Judge Robb voted for dismissal on the basis that the case presented a nonjusticiable political question. Under his position, federal courts would not be able to determine the legal status of international terrorism nor trace individual responsibility for any particular acts of terrorism. In addition, given the levels of violence in the world, Robb was not convinced that there was any logical stopping point to litigation that could be pursued in the United States.

6. Forti v. Suarez-Mason, 672 F. Supp. 1531 (N.D. Cal. 1987), *aff'd in part*, 694 F. Supp. 707 (N.D. Cal. 1988); Martinez-Baca v. Suarez-Mason, No. 87–2057 (N.D. Cal. April 22, 1988); Quiros de Rapaport v. Suarez-Mason, No. C87–2266 (N.D. Cal. April 11, 1989).

7. Xuncax v. Gramajo and Ortiz v. Gramajo, 886 F. Supp. 162 (D. Mass. 1995).

8. 72 F. 3d 844 (11th Cir. 1996).

9. Paul v. Avril, 812 F. Supp. 207 (S.D. Fla. 1992) *aff'd*, 901 F. Supp. 330 (S.D. Fla. 1994).

10. Belance v. FRAPH, No. 94–2619 (E.D.N.Y. filed June 1, 1994).

11. No. 92–122555, 1994 WL 827111 (D. Mass. October 26, 1994).

12. Mushikiwabo v. Barayagwiza, No. 94–3627, 1996 WL 164496 (S.D.N.Y. Apr., 9, 1996).

13. 866 F. Supp. 734 (S.D.N.Y. 1994), *rev'd*, 70 F. 3d 232 (2d Cir. 1995).

14. Trajano v. Marcos, 978 F. 2d 493 (9th Cir. 1992).

15. Linda Greenhouse, "Reviewing Foreigners' Use of Federal Courts," *New York Times*, December 2, 2003, A22.

16. See Foreign Relations Authorization Act, Fiscal Year 1994 and 1995, Pub. L. No. 103–236, § 506 (a), 108 Stat. 382, 463–64 (1994) (codified at 18 U.S.C. § 2340).

17. Convention against Torture and Other Cruel, Inhuman or Degrading Treatment. Done at New York, December 10, 1984. Entered into force, June 26, 1987. U.N. G.A. Res. 39/46 Annex, 39 U.N. GAOR, Supp. (No. 51) 197, U.N. Doc. E/CN.4/1984/72, Annex (1984).

18. William Schulz, "The Torturers among Us," *New York Review of Books*, April 15, 2002.

19. Article 7 of the Torture Convention reads: "The State Party in the territory whose jurisdiction a person alleged to have committed [torture] shall in the cases contemplated . . . , if it does not extradite him, submit the case to its competent authorities for the purpose of prosecution.

20. Pub. L. No. 102–256, 106 Stat. 73 (1992) (codified at 28 U.S.C. 1350 note).

21. The exceptions are essentially as follows: if a state has waived

its immunity; if the cause of action relates to "commercial activities" engaged in by the state; if the case involves property that is taken in violation of international law; or if the state commits a "tortious act" in the United States. 28 U.S.C. § 1605.

22. The result would have been different if the torture, or the "tortious acts," had been carried out in the United States instead. The leading case in this area is *Letelier v. Chile*, 488 F. Supp. 665 (D.D.C. 1980), which was a suit brought against Chile alleging that the Chilean government had hired foreign agents (Cuban agents to be exact) who detonated a bomb in Washington, D.C., that killed Orlando Letelier, a former Chilean ambassador to the United States, and Ronni Moffit, Letelier's assistant.

23. 28 U.S.C. § 1605 (a)(7) (1994).

24. 28 U.S.C. §§ 1330, 1602–11 (1994).

25. *Alejandre v. Cuba*, 996 F. Supp. 1239 (S.D. Fla. 1997) was a suit brought by the personal representatives of three people who died as a result of the shooting down of two unarmed civilian planes over international waters by the Cuban Air Force.

26. Daliberti v. Republic of Iraq, No. 96–1118, 2000 WL 68413 (D.D.C. May 23, 2000).

27. In *Flatlow v. Iran*, 999 F. Supp. 1 (D.D.C. 1998), the plaintiff alleged that his daughter was the victim of a terrorist suicide bombing of an Israeli bus on which his daughter was a passenger. The Shaqiqi faction of Palestine Islamic Jihad claimed responsibility for the bombing, and investigations by the U.S. Department of State confirmed this claim. The State Department also reported that Iran had provided approximately $2 million annually to the Palestine Islamic Jihad for support of international terrorist activities. In doing so, at least according to the U.S. court, Iran had provided the requisite "material support" and thus could be held civilly liable to the Flatlow family.

In *Cicippio v. Iran*, 18 F. Supp. 2d 62 (D.D.C. 1998), the U.S. District Court for the District of Columbia ordered the government of Iran to pay a total of $65 million to Joseph Cicippio and two other plaintiffs who were abducted at gunpoint by Hezbollah agents during 1985–1986 and held hostage for periods ranging from a year and a half to over five years, as well as to the wives of two of the former hostages for the suffering they endured while their husbands were in captivity.

28. Allison Taylor, "Another Front on the War on Terrorism? Problems with Recent Changes to the Foreign Sovereign Immunities Act," *Arizona Law Review* 45 (2003): 533–58.

29. One possibility, of course, is the newly created International

Criminal Court (ICC), although it is important to note that under the ICC, private individuals will not be able to initiate legal proceedings.

30. Or better yet, if in addition to the International Criminal Court there were created an International *Civil* Court through which individuals would be empowered to enforce their own rights against those states that were responsible for carrying out human rights violations against them. See Mark Gibney, "On the Need for an International Civil Court," *Fletcher Forum of World Affairs* 26 (2002): 47–58 (2002).

31. 568 F. Supp. (D.D.C. 1983), *aff'd*, 770 F. 2d 202 (D.C. Cir. 1985).

32. Brief for the Appellants at 7, Sanchez-Espinoza v. Reagan, 770 F. Supp. 202 (D.C. Cir. 1985) (citations omitted) (copy with author).

33. The Supreme Court held: "In order to adjudicate the tort claims of the Nicaraguan plaintiffs, we would have to determine the precise nature of the United States government's involvement in the affairs of several Central American nations, namely, Honduras, Costa Rica, El Salvador, and Nicaragua." 568 F. Supp. at 601.

34. 770 F. 2d at 207 (citations and emphasis omitted).

35. *Id.* at 208.

36. Scalia writes:

Whether or not the present litigation is motivated by considerations of geopolitics rather than personal harm, we think that as a general matter the danger of foreign citizens' [sic] using the courts in situations such as this to obstruct the foreign policy of our government is sufficiently acute that we must leave to Congress the judgment whether a damage remedy should exist.

Id. at 209.

37. 707 F. Supp. 319 (D.D.C. 1988).

38. *Id.* at 322.

39. *Id.*

40. *Id.*

41. *Id.*

42. 1991 WL 43262 (D.D.C. 1991) *aff'd*, 971 F. 2d 766 (D.C. Cir. 1992).

43. Sigrun Skogly and Mark Gibney, "Transnational Human Rights Obligations," *Human Rights Quarterly* 24 (2002): 781–98.

44. Case Concerning Military and Paramilitary Activities in and against Nicaragua (Nicaragua v. United States), 1986 I.C.J. Reports, 14 (June 27, 1986).

45. Among the violations committed by agents of the United States were the following: By training, arming, equipping, financing, and sup-

plying the Contra rebel forces, the United States had violated the obligation not to intervene in the affairs of another state. Through its actions in armed attacks at various locations in Nicaragua, the United States had breached its obligation under customary international law not to use force against another state. And in laying mines in the internal and territorial waters of Nicaragua, the United States was in breach of its obligations under customary international law not to use force against another state, not to intervene in its affairs, not to violate its sovereignty, and not to interrupt peaceful maritime commerce.

46. Military and Paramilitary Activities, note 44, par. 106 (emphasis supplied).

47. The extraordinarily high standard for transnational state responsibility set forth in *Nicaragua v. United States* has seemingly been tempered by the Appeals Chamber of the International Criminal Tribunal for the Former Yugoslavia in its *Tadic* decision, which rejected the "effective control" standard used by the ICJ in the *Nicaragua* case. Recognizing that "the whole body of international law on State responsibility is based on a realistic concept of accountability," the Appeals Chamber employed a much lower "overall control" standard with respect to military or paramilitary groups, while for reasons that were never fully explained, the Supreme Court was of the opinion that a higher standard was warranted when the controlling state is not the territorial state where the armed clashes occur. Prosecutor v. Dusko Tadic, in *The Appeals Chamber of the International Tribunal for the Prosecution of Persons Responsible for Serious Violations of International Humanitarian Law Committed in the Territory of the Former Yugoslavia since 1991*, Judgment of July 15, 1999, www.un.org.icty/tadic/appeal/judgement/tad-aj990715e.htm.

48. See, generally, Mark Gibney, Katarina Tomasevski, and Jens Vedsted-Hansen, "Transnational State Responsibility for Violations of Human Rights," *Harvard Human Rights Journal* 12 (1999): 267–95.

49. 724 F. Supp. 753 (C.D. Cal. 1989).

50. *Id.* at 755.

51. 976 F. 2d at 1131.

52. *Id.*

53. 175 U.S. 677 (1900). The case involved the seizure of two Spanish fishing vessels by United States naval forces engaged in a military blockade during the Spanish–American War. The Court ruled that the decision to seize the vessels was not justified by military necessity and that the vessels must be returned.

54. 976 F. 2d at 1332.

55. *Id.*

56. The plaintiffs sued under a number of federal statutes. However, nearly all the court's analysis focused on the Federal Tort Claims Act, 28 U.S.C. § 1346 (b).

57. 28 U.S.C. § 2674 (1988).

58. 28 U.S.C. § 2680 (j).

59. 976 F. 2d at 1334–35.

60. *Id.* at 1335.

61. The court's rationale was as follows:

> There can be no doubt that during the "tanker war" a "time of war" existed. The United States' involvement in naval combat while the Iran–Iraq war was in progress was the result of a deliberate decision on the part of the executive branch to engage in hostile military activities vis-à-vis Iran in order to protect Gulf shipping. Our activities included not only the defense of re-flagged tankers servicing Iraq's needs, but ultimately attacks upon Iranian gunboats and oil platforms. The Vincennes' actions constituted a part of our military involvement in the Persian Gulf. The act of shooting down the Iranian civilian aircraft, although a tragic error, was committed in order to further the perceived interests of the United States in its involvement in the tanker war. Moreover, we believe that the ill-fated Iranian Airbus may fairly be said to have been operating "during time of war" both temporally and spatially. The aircraft took off from an Iranian airport used for both civilian and military purposes. Its flight path was in the general area in which hostilities had occurred with regularity over the past year. The United States had issued warning to all aircraft operations in the region notifying them of the dangers. The pilots of the Iranian aircraft should not have been surprised to encounter conditions of "war." Under the circumstances, we believe that the shooting down of the Airbus by the Vincennes falls within the FTCA's exception for combatant activities during time of war. Accordingly, the plaintiffs' FTCA action against the Vincennes is barred by the doctrine of sovereign immunity.

Id. at 1335.

62. See, generally, Ethan A. Nadelmann, *Cops across Borders: The Internationalization of U.S. Criminal Law Enforcement* (University Park: The Pennsylvania State University Press, 1993).

63. The other side to this occurred in April 2001 when an airplane carrying American missionaries to Latin America was downed when Peruvian drug enforcement agents mistakenly believed that the plane

was being used for drug-running purposes. Irvin Molotsky, "Baptists' Plane Was Identified as Drug Carrier," *New York Times*, April 22, 2001, A1.

64. "Civilian Toll in Fog of War: Civilian Deaths in Afghanistan," *New York Times*, February 10, 2002, A1; Carlotta Gall, "Released Afghans Tell of Beatings," *New York Times*, February 11, 2002, A1; Thom Shaker and James Risen, "U.S. Troops Search for Clues to Victims of Missile Strike," *New York Times*, February 11, 2002, A12; Thom Shanker, "U.S. Says 16 Killed in Raids Weren't Taliban or Al Qaeda," *New York Times*, February 22, 2002, A1; Carlotta Gall, "Afghan Villagers Torn by Grief After U.S. Raid Kills 9 Children," *New York Times*, December 8, 2003, A1; Carlotta Gall, "Afghan Children Again Die as U.S. Strikes at Taliban," *New York Times*, December 11, 2003, A3.

65. David M. Halbfinger, "Unusual Factors Converge in Case against War Pilots," *New York Times*, January 25, 2003, A9.

66. "National Briefing: South; Louisiana; Lesser Charges in Bombing," *New York Times*, July 1, 2003, A20.

67. 976 F. 2d at 1335.

68. See generally, Harold Hongju Koh, "How the President (Almost) Always Wins in Foreign Affairs: Lessons of the Iran-Contra Affair," *Yale Law Journal* (1988): 1255–1342; Louis Henkin, *Foreign Affairs and the Constitution*, 2d ed. (Oxford: Clarendon Press, 1996).

69. 859 F. 2d 929, 941 (D.C. Cir. 1988) (emphasis supplied).

70. John Rawls, *A Theory of Justice* (Cambridge, MA: Harvard University Press, 1971).

71. As we saw in the previous chapter, however, the Fourth Amendment does not offer very much protection to foreign nationals.

72. The name comes from *Bivens v. Six Unknown Agents*, 403 U.S. 388 (1971) where the Supreme Court allowed individuals who were subjected to particularly egregious violations committed by federal officials to sue for monetary damages under the Fourteenth Amendment.

73. Federal Tort Claims Act, note 56.

74. Seymour M. Hersh, "A Case Not Closed," *New Yorker*, November 1, 1993.

75. Eric Schmitt, "U.S. Says Strike Crippled Iraq's Capacity for Terror," *New York Times*, June 28, 1993, A1.

NOTES TO CHAPTER 4

1. Susan D. Moeller, *Compassion Fatigue: How the Media Sell Disease, Famine, War and Death* (New York: Routledge, 1999).

2. Thomas Pogge, *World Poverty and Human Rights: Cosmopolitan Responsibilities and Reform* (Malden, MA: Polity, 2002), 5.

3. For an excellent discussion of the dual worlds of refugee protection see Jacqueline Bhabha, "Internationalist Gatekeepers? The Tension between Asylum Advocacy and Human Rights," *Harvard Human Rights Journal* 15 (2002): 155–81. Also in the same journal, see the introduction, "Boundaries in the Field of Human Rights."

4. This is not to say that I endorse "open borders." In fact, in many ways I support the opposite policy. In my view, states should maintain strict control over entry, but they should also establish—and follow—priorities for admission that are based on principles of law, justice, and need. Like Michael Walzer, I believe that those with the strongest basis for admission are those whom we have helped turn into refugees. Mark Gibney, *Strangers or Friends: Principles for a New Alien Admission Policy* (Westport, CT: Greenwood Press, 1986).

5. One of the very few scholars to even test this proposition is Joseph Carens, "Nationalism and the Exclusion of Immigrants: Lessons from Australian Immigration Policy," in *Open Borders? Closed Societies? The Ethical and Political Issues*, ed. Mark Gibney (Westport, CT: Greenwood Press, 1988).

6. The Human Rights Watch Arms Project has published a number of important studies documenting the arms selling that goes on in some of the most volatile areas in the world. Among those reports are the following: "Stoking the Fires: Military Assistance and Arms Trafficking in Burundi" (1997); "Rwanda/Zaire: Rearming with Impunity: International Support for the Perpetrators of the Rwandan Genocide" (1995); "Angola: Between War and Peace—Arms Trade and Human Rights Abuses Since the Lusaka Protocol" (1996).

7. See, generally, Edward S. Herman, "The United States versus Human Rights in the Third World," *Harvard Human Rights Journal* 4 (1991): 85–104; Christopher B. Jochnick and Josh Zimmer, "The Day of the Dictator: Zaire's Mobutu and United States Foreign Policy," *Harvard Human Rights Journal* 4 (1991): 139–51.

8. Daan Bronkhorst has done one of the leading studies in this area, and what he finds is enormous variability throughout Europe, which leads to questions of accuracy and consistency. For example, at the time of his study, Turkish asylum seekers in Germany had an acceptance rate in the Netherlands that was six times higher than in Germany. Similarly, while Tamils had virtually no chance of being admitted as refugees in the Netherlands or Germany, a broad majority were granted refugee status in France. In Denmark, Somalis had a much better rate of acceptance than Turks, while in the Netherlands

it was the other way around. In the United Kingdom, Ethiopians fared somewhat better than Iraqis, while in Germany Ethiopians had only half the chance of Iraqis. Daan Bronkhurst, "The Realism of a European Asylum Policy: A Quantitative Approach," *Netherlands Quarterly of Human Rights* 2 (1991): 142–58.

9. Convention Relating to the Status of Refugees. Done at Geneva, July 28, 1951. Entered into force, April 22, 1954. 189 U.N.T.S. (United Nations Treaty Series) 137.

10. Two regional conventions—one for Africa and one for Latin America—explicitly include in their definition of "refugee" those fleeing violence. The Organization of African Unity (OAU) Convention governing the specific aspects of refugee problems in Africa, U.N.T.S. 14,691, entered into force June 20, 1974, uses the same kind of language that the UN definition does, but also adds the following:

> The term refugee shall also apply to every person who, owing to external aggression, occupation, foreign domination or events seriously disturbing public order in either part or the whole of his country of origin or nationality, is compelled to leave his place of habitual residence in order to seek refuge in another place outside his country of origin or nationality.

The so-called Cartegena Declaration, adopted by ten Latin American States in 1984, employs the Convention definition, and then this additional language:

> persons who have fled their country because their lives, safety, or freedom have been threatened by a generalized violence, foreign aggression, internal conflicts, massive violations of human rights or other circumstances which have seriously disturbed public order.

Annual Report of Inter-American Commission on Human Rights 1984–1985, OEA/Ser.L/II.66, doc. 10, rev. 1, conclusion 3.

11. This description comes from a very influential article by David Martin, "Reforming Asylum Adjudication: On Navigating the Coast of Bohemia," *University of Pennsylvania Law Review* 138 (1990): 1247–1381, 1367.

12. The situation for Nicaraguans was treated differently after 1986 based on the idea that asylum seekers from Nicaragua were attempting to escape from the "totalitarian" Sandinista regime.

13. Mark Gibney, "A 'Well-Founded Fear' of Persecution," *Human Rights Quarterly* 10 (1988): 109–21; Mark Gibney et al., "USA Refugee Policy: A Human Rights Analysis Update," *Journal of Refugee Studies* 5

(1992): 33–46; Mark Gibney, "In Search of a U.S. Refugee Policy," in *The United States and Human Rights: Looking Inward and Outward*, ed. David Forsythe (Lincoln: University of Nebraska Press, 2000).

14. 502 U.S. 478 (1992).

15. *Id.* at 483.

16. *Id.* (emphasis in original).

17. Article 33 (par. 1) of the Refugee Convention, 189 U.N.T.S. 137, reads: "No Contracting State shall expel or return ("refouler") a refugee in any manner whatsoever to the frontiers or territories where his life or freedom would be threatened on account of his race, religion, nationality, membership of a particular social group or political opinion."

18. 509 U.S. 155 (1993).

19. Thomas Alexander Alienikoff, David Martin, and Hiroshi Motomura, *Immigration and Citizenship: Process and Policy*, 4th ed. (St. Paul, MN: West Group, 1998), 1158.

20. Immigration and Nationality Act § 241 (b) (3) reads: "[T]he Attorney General may not remove an alien to a country if the Attorney General decides that the alien's life or freedom would be threatened in that country because of the alien's race, religion, nationality, membership in a particular social group, or political opinion."

21. For an excellent critique of European asylum practices see Maryellen Fullerton, "Failing the Test: Germany Leads Europe in Dismantling Refugee Protection," *Texas International Law Journal* 36 (2001): 231–75.

22. Guy Goodwin-Gill, "Safe Country? Says Who?" *International Journal of Refugee Law* 4 (1992): 248–50.

23. Michael Walzer, *Spheres of Justice: A Defense of Pluralism and Equality* (New York: Basic Books, 1983), 49.

24. As David Martin has pointed out, the much different manner in which asylum seekers now arrive has made it that much easier to question the claims being presented. Under the old system, individuals would first flee their country of origin and then reside for some time (perhaps a decade or more) in an austere refugee camp before resettlement came about (assuming that it ever did). While this process was quite harsh for those who were forced to live through it, it did serve a decidedly useful purpose for receiving countries: the privations that these individuals lived through provided "us" with a strong assurance of their claims. As Martin goes on to say, the same thing is not true today in the era of "jet-set" refugees (although this greatly overestimates the number of asylum seekers who arrive by air, at least in the United States). In essence, asylum seekers are no longer given any kind of benefit of the doubt. In fact, quite the opposite is true: their claims

are met with enormous levels of suspicion—by policymakers and the public alike. David Martin, "The New Asylum Seekers," in *The New Asylum Seekers: Refugee Law in the 1980s*, ed. David Martin (Dordrecht, the Netherlands: Martinus Nijhoff Publishers, 1986).

25. The numbers of refugees who have been admitted to the United States over the past two decades through the overseas admission program have been as follows (note the severe decline over the course of the past two decades): 1980 (207,116), 1981 (159,252), 1982 (97,355), 1983 (61,681), 1984 (71,113), 1985 (68,045), 1986 (62,440), 1987 (64,828), 1988 (76,487), 1989 (107,238), 1990 (122,326), 1991 (112,811), 1992 (132,173), 1993 (119,482), 1994 (112,682), 1995 (99,490), 1996 (75,693), 1997 (70,085), 1998 (76,554), 1999 (85,006) and 2000 (72,515). Following September 11, only 27,000 of the 70,000 refugees who were scheduled to arrive in the United States actually were admitted—the lowest number in a quarter century. The quota for fiscal year 2003 was lowered to 50,000, but still, only 28,000 refugees were resettled in the United States. The long backlog has resulted in forced confinement in foreign camps under extraordinarily inhospitable conditions, as tens of thousands wait for an entry into the United States that might never come about. Rachel L. Swarns, "U.S. Security Concerns Trap Thousands in Kenyan Camp," *New York Times*, January 29, 2003, A3.

26. See note 13.

27. Pub. L. 105–118, § 574, 111 Stat. 2386, 2432 (1997). The amendment was first adopted by Congress in 1989, and it provides that certain categories of individuals from Communist (or former Communist) countries are deemed to satisfy the well-founded fear standard merely by "asserting" such a fear and by asserting a "credible basis" for concern about the possibility of such persecution. The statutory language requires the attorney general to establish one or more categories of people from the former Soviet Union, Vietnam, Laos, and Cambodia who "share common characteristics that identify them as targets of persecution." People in these categories would enjoy the benefit of the lower evidentiary burden. In fact, the statute itself specifically provides for certain categories including Jews, Evangelical Christians, and Ukrainian Catholics or Ukrainian Orthodox from the former Soviet Union.

28. Susan Raufer, "In Country Processing of Refugees," *Georgetown Immigration Law Journal* 9 (1995): 233–62.

29. Priority One reads as follows:

The following UNHCR-referred or U.S. embassy identified cases: persons facing compelling security concerns in countries of first asylum; persons in need of legal protection because of the danger of refoulement; those in danger due to threats of armed attack in areas where they are located; persons who have experienced persecution because of their political, religious, or human rights activities; women-at-risk; victims of torture or violence; physically or mentally disabled persons; persons in urgent need of medical attention not available in the first asylum country; and persons for whom other durable solutions are not feasible and whose status in the place of asylum does not present a satisfactory long-term solution.

Priority Two is for people belonging to U.S. Department of State–identified refugee groups in consultation with nongovernmental organizations (NGOs), United Nations High Commission for Refugees (UNHCR), the Immigration and Naturalization Service (INS), and other area experts. Priorities Three through Five provide for the admission of refugees who have relatives in the United States including uncles, aunts, nieces, nephews, first cousins, and so on. U.S. Committee for Refugees, *Refugee Reports*, vol. 20 (1999).

30. "Better Conditions Sought for Chechen Refugees," *New York Times*, January 17, 2002, A9 (upward of 180,000 Chechen refugees are spending their third straight winter homeless).

31. Or as a recent editorial in the *New York Times* stated it: "Priorities for entry are still tilted toward the Cold War—one of the largest groups admitted, for example, is Jews from the former Soviet Union, not among those in the most dire need today." Editorial, "Closing Doors to Refugees," *New York Times*, February 19, 2002, A22.

32. The last year for large numbers was 1995, when the United States admitted 33,214 Vietnamese "refugees." The numbers then went to 17,021 (1996), 7,469 (1997), 10,661 (1998), 9,863 (1999), and 3,845 (2000).

33. The numbers from Bosnia are as follows: 0 (1993), 7,197 (1994), 9,870 (1995), 12,030 (1996), 21,357 (1997), 30,906 (1998), 22,697 (1999), and 19,027 (2000).

34. See note 13.

35. See note 25.

NOTES TO CHAPTER 5

1. The Program on International Policy, "Americans on Foreign Aid and World Hunger: A Study of U.S. Public Attitudes," www.pipa.org [accessed March 9, 2004].

2. Only one-third of U.S. foreign aid goes to states that have been designated as Low-Income Countries. *The Reality of Aid: An Independent Review of Poverty Reduction and Development Assistance* (London: Earthscan, 1998), 77.

3. *The Reality of Aid*, 77, 103.

4. Barbara Crossette, "U.S. Foreign Aid Budget: Quick, How Much? Wrong." *New York Times*, January 27, 1995, A4; "Foreign Aid: Under Siege in the Budget Wars," *New York Times*, April 30, 1995, E4.

5. "Foreign Aid: Under Siege in the Budget Wars," *New York Times*, April 30, 1995, E4.

6. Riley E. Dunlop, "Americans Have Positive Image of the Environmental Movement," The Gallup Organization, April 18, 2000, www.gallup.com/poll/releases/pr000418.asp [accessed March 9, 2004].

7. Andrew C. Revkin, "Warming Threat Requires Action Now, Scientists Say," *New York Times*, June 12, 2001, A12.

8. "We Leave More than Footprints," *National Geographic*, July 2001.

9. This is the major thesis of Donald A. Brown's book *American Heat: Ethical Problems with the United States' Response to Global Warming* (Lanham, MD: Rowman & Littlefield, 2002).

10. White House spokesperson Ari Fleischer described our "rights" in this way: "The American way of life is a blessed one. We have a bounty of resources in this country. What we need to do is make certain that we're able to get those resources . . . into the hands of consumers so they can make the choices that they want to make as they live their daily lives." Quoted in Paul Krugman, "Nation in a Jam," *New York Times*, May 13, 2001, sec. 4, 13.

11. Bill McKibben, "An End to Sweet Illusions," *Mother Jones* (January/February 2002): 39.

12. The *New York Times* headline says it all: Andrew C. Revkin, "178 Nations Reach a Climate Accord: U.S. Only Looks On," *New York Times*, July 24, 2001, A1.

13. Andrew Revkin, "Climate Changing, U.S. Says in Report," *New York Times*, June 3, 2002, A1.

14. Gary Gardner, "The Challenge for Johannesburg: Creating a More Secure World," The World Watch Institute, *State of the World 2002* (New York: Norton, 2002), 5.

15. Quoted in Tami R. Davis and Sean M. Lynn-Jones, "A Citty on the Hill," *Foreign Policy* 66 (1987): 20–38.

16. Ben J. Wattenberg, *The Good News Is the Bad News Is Wrong* (New York: Simon & Schuster, 1984), 362.

17. Juan Mendez has argued that the reason why the war on terror-

ism is such a hollow concept in much of the world is that the United States simply pushes aside its own past practices. He writes:

Even when the United States criticizes policies of repressive governments (or of repressive actors and institutions in democratic governments), public opinion in those countries often distrusts the intentions of different American administrations. This in turn conspires to limit the effectiveness of Americans statements and measures. One reason for this distrust is that American officials almost never acknowledge any history of past American support for those repressive state agents or institutions. Year after year, the State Department acts as if it was writing on a clean slate, especially when it comes to U.S. support for repressive regimes in the past.

Juan Mendez, "Human Rights Policy in the Age of Terrorism," *Saint Louis University Law Journal* 46 (2002): 377–403, 400 (footnotes omitted).

18. Nicholas D. Kristof, "Our Own Terrorist," *New York Times*, March 5, 2002, A25.

19. See, generally, Iain Guest, *Behind the Disappearances: Argentina's Dirty War against Human Rights and the United Nations* (Philadelphia: University of Pennsylvania Press, 1990).

20. Lawrence Weschler, *A Miracle, a Universe: Settling Accounts with Torturers* (New York: Pantheon, 1990), 62.

21. This is not meant to underplay the atrocities committed by the U.S. government itself. Between March 1969 and August 1973, U.S. planes dropped 540,000 tons of bombs on the Cambodian countryside and U.S. B-52 raids killed tens of thousands of civilians. Samantha Power, *"A Problem from Hell": America and the Age of Genocide* (New York: Basic Books, 2002), 94.

22. William Shawcross, *Sideshow: Kissinger, Nixon and the Destruction of Cambodia* (New York: Simon & Schuster), 396.

23. Christopher Hitchens, "The Case against Henry Kissinger (Part Two)," *Harper's Magazine*, March 2001, 49.

24. Mark Ensalaco, *Chile under Pinochet: Recovering the Truth* (Philadelphia: University of Pennsylvania Press, 2000), 156–57.

25. Robin Kirk, *More Terrible than Death: Massacres, Drugs, and America's War in Colombia* (New York: Public Affairs, 2003), xv–xvi.

26. Hitchens, "The Case against Henry Kissinger," 58.

27. Christopher Hitchens, "Kissinger's Green Light to Suharto," *Nation*, February 18, 2002, 9.

28. Allan Nairn, "U.S. Complicity in Timor," *Nation*, September 27, 1999, 5.

29. Clifford Kraus, "U.S., Aware of Killings, Worked with Salvadoran's Rightists, Papers Suggest," *New York Times*, November 9, 1993, A4; Tim Weiner, "Documents Assert U.S. Trained Salvadorans Tied to Death Squads," *New York Times*, December 14, 1993, A1; Clifford Kraus, "How U.S. Actions Helped Hide Salvador Human Rights Abuses," *New York Times*, March 21, 1993, A1.

30. See Mark Danner, *The Massacre at El Mozote: A Parable of the Cold War* (New York: Vintage Books, 1994).

31. Theodore A. Couloumbis, *The United States, Greece and Turkey: The Troubled Triangle* (New York: Praeger Press, 1983), 50–55.

32. Sam Dillon and Tim Weiner, "In Guatemala's Dark Heart, C.I.A. Tied to Death and Aid," *New York Times*, April 2, 1995, A1; Mireya Navarro, "Guatemala Study Accuses the Army and Cites U.S. Role," *New York Times*, February 26, 1999, A1.

33. Alison Acker, *Honduras: The Making of a Banana Republic* (Boston: South End Press, 1988), 109–30.

34. Jonathan Kwitny, *Endless Enemies: The Making of an Unfriendly World* (New York: Penguin Books, 1984), 281.

35. Stephen Kinzer, *All the Shah's Men: An American Coup and the Roots of Middle East Terror* (Hoboken, NJ: Wiley, 2003).

36. Power, *"A Problem from Hell,"* chap. 8.

37. Charles J. Hanley, Sang-Hun Choe, and Martha Mendoza, *The Bridge at No Gun Ri: A Hidden Nightmare from the Korean War* (New York: Henry Holt, 2001).

38. Howard W. French, "South Koreans Seek Truth about '48 Massacre," *New York Times*, October 24, 2001, A3.

39. Roger Warner, *Shooting at the Moon: The Story of America's Clandestine War in Laos* (South Royalton, VT: Steerforth Press, 1996), 380.

40. Warner, *Shooting at the Moon*, 381.

41. John Dinges, *Our Man in Panama: How General Noriega Used the U.S.—and Made Millions in Drugs and Arms* (New York: Random House, 1990), 318.

42. Diana Jean Schemo, "Archives Unearthed in Paraguay Expose U.S. Allies' Abuses," *New York Times*, August 11, 1999, A1.

43. Mark Twain, " 'Thirty Thousand Killed a Million,' " *Atlantic Monthly*, April 1992, 52.

44. Raymond Bonner, *Waltzing with a Dictator: The Marcoses and the Making of American Policy* (New York: Times Books, 1987).

45. Philip Gourevitch, *We Wish to Inform You That Tomorrow We Will Be Killed with Our Families: Stories from Rwanda* (New York: Picador, 1998), 149–50.

46. Richard Payne, *The Nonsuperpowers and South Africa: Implications for U.S. Policy* (Bloomington: Indiana University Press, 1990), 247.

47. John Tirman, *Spoils of War: The Human Consequences of America's Arms Trade* (New York: Free Press, 1997).

48. Weschler, *A Miracle, a Universe*, 118–19.

49. Kwitny, *Endless Enemies*, 61–62.

50. Kwitny, *Endless Enemies*, 63.

51. What I am referring to here in particular is what has been termed Carter's Malaise Speech, where he suggested that the United States was afflicted with a certain "malaise." Toward the end of his speech Carter states:

> We are at a turning point in our history. There are two paths to choose. One is a path I've warned about tonight, the path that leads to fragmentation and self-interest. Down that road lies a mistaken idea of freedom, the right to grasp for ourselves some advantage over others. That path would be one of constant conflict between narrow interests ending in chaos and immobility. It is a certain route to failure. All the traditions of our past, all the lessons of our heritage, all the promises of our future point to another path, the path of common purpose and the restoration of American values. That path leads to true freedom for our Nation and ourselves.

Public condemnation came from all quarters. Carter had violated the cardinal sin of American politics: never criticize the United States or its people. Still, what is most noteworthy has been Carter's work after leaving office and the worldwide respect and admiration that he enjoys, culminating in being awarded the 2002 Nobel Peace Prize.

NOTES TO CHAPTER 6

1. One of the most noteworthy and controversial domestic apologies has really been a nonapology. The Australian government, under the leadership of Conservative prime minister John Howard, has steadfastly refused to issue an apology for the ill-treatment of the country's Aboriginal population, although the government has issued a Declaration Towards Reconciliation and established various restitution schemes. Clyde Farnsworth, "Facing Pain of Aborigines Wrested from Families, Many Australians Shrug," *New York Times*, June 8, 1997, A10. The decision not to apologize (but to take measures just short of this) can often be explained based on the dynamics of domestic politics. Needless

to say, however, the battle over whether an apology should be given (or whether an apology actually has been given) oftentimes tends to reignite old passions and does much to subvert the entire enterprise. As I explain later, the preferred course is to ask for forgiveness rather than issuing a unilateral apology that does not really include those who have been harmed.

2. Of all the former colonial powers, Great Britain has progressed the furthest in terms of coming to terms with its past. In 1995, Queen Elizabeth issued a strongly worded apology to the indigenous Maori tribes in New Zealand. The apology acknowledged that the crown had acted "unjustly," and that the British army's role had a "crippling impact" on Maori life. The apology goes on to state: "The Crown expresses its profound regret and apologizes unreservedly for the loss of lives because of hostilities arising from this invasion and at the devastation of property and social life which resulted."

The apology also admits to colonial mistakes, offers compensation for land that was unlawfully confiscated, and goes so far as to describe colonial policy as a "crime." Elazar Barkan, *The Guilt of Nations: Restitution and Negotiating Historical Injustices* (New York: Norton, 2000), 264.

Since then, however, the British government has become much more timid, in large part because of a concern with the legal implications of opening up a Pandora's box of colonial atrocities. These measures include Prime Minister Tony Blair's expression of "remorse" for Great Britain's role in the Potato Famine in Ireland. His feelings are expressed in the form of a letter that was read by the Irish actor Gabriel Byrne at the close of events commemorating the famine. In the letter Blair writes:

> Those who governed in London at the time failed their people through standing by while a crop failure turned into a massive human tragedy. That one million people died in what was then part of the richest and most powerful nation in the world is something that still causes pain as we reflect on it today.

Sarah Lyall, "Past as Prologue: Blair Faults Britain in Irish Potato Blight," *New York Times*, June 3, 1997, A3.

An even weaker effort was Queen Elizabeth's participation at a ceremony at Jallianwala Bagh in the Indian city of Amritsar honoring the victims of a British attack on April 13, 1919. The Queen attended the ceremony but had been instructed by the government not to utter a word, lest legal consequences would flow from the admission of wrongdoing. John Burns, "In India, Queen Bows Her Head over a Massacre in 1919," *New York Times*, October 15, 1997, A6. Finally, in November 1999 in Pretoria, South Africa, Queen Elizabeth voiced "sadness" over the loss of life in the Boer War, but she stopped short of issuing a full apology as demanded by many Afrikaner groups. "Expression of Sorrow, but No Apology," *New York Times*, November 11, 1999, A3.

3. No doubt the most widely publicized religious apologies have been those issued by Pope John Paul II in spring 2000. The first was during a Sunday liturgy where he, along with seven cardinals and bishops, cited a number of Church lapses, past and present, including religious intolerance and injustice toward Jews, women, indigenous peoples, immigrants, the poor, and the unborn. The Pope's apology included the following lamentations:

> We cannot not recognize the betrayals of the Gospel committed by some of our brothers, especially during the second millennium. We ask forgiveness for the divisions between Christians, for the use of violence that some have resorted to in the service of truth and for the acts of dissidence and of hostility sometimes taken towards followers of other religions.
>
> We confess to our responsibilities as Christians for the sins of today. Before atheism, religious indifference, secularism, ethical relativism, to violations of the right to life, to the indifference towards poverty of many countries, we cannot not ask ourselves what are our responsibilities.

Alessandra Stanley, "Pope Asks Forgiveness for Errors of the Church over 2,000 Years," *New York Times*, March 13, 2000, A1. After this, the Pope issued an apology at Yad Vashem, the saddest and starkest memorial in Israel, for the role played by the Church during the Holocaust. Included in his apology was the following:

> I have come to Yad Vashem to pay homage to the millions of Jewish people who, stripped of everything, especially of their human dignity, were murdered in the Holocaust. More than a half century has passed, but the memories remain.
>
> Here, as in Auschwitz and many other places in Europe, we are overcome by the echo of the heart-rendering laments of so many. Men, women, children cry out to us from the depths of the horror that they knew. How can we fail to heed their cry? No one can forget or ignore what happened. No one can diminish its scale. We wish to remember. But we wish to remember for a purpose, namely to ensure that never again will evil prevail as it did for the millions of innocent victims of Nazism.

NOTES TO CHAPTER 6

How could man have such utter contempt for man? Because we had reached the point of contempt for God. Only a Godless ideology could plan and carry out the extermination of a whole people.

As Bishop of Rome and successor of the Apostle Peter, I assure the Jewish people that the Catholic Church, motivated by the Gospel of truth and love and by no political considerations, is deeply saddened by the hatred, acts of persecution and displays of anti-Semitism directed against the Jews by Christians at any time and in any place. The Church rejects racism in any form as a denial of the image of the Creator inherent in every human being.

In this place of solemn remembrance, I fervently pray that our sorrow for the tragedy which the Jewish people suffered in the 20th century will lead to a new relationship between Christians and Jews. Let us build a new future in which there will be no more anti-Jewish feeling among Christians, or anti-Christian feeling among Jews, but rather the mutual respect required of those who adore the one Creator and Lord, and look to Abraham as our common father in faith.

Alessandra Stanley, "At Yad Vashem, Pope Tries to Salve History's Scars," *New York Times*, March 24, 2000, A1. In May 2001 the Pope expressed "deep regret" for the misdeeds committed against the Greek Orthodox Church, especially during the Crusades. Alessandra Stanley, "In Athens, Pope Voices Regret for Church Sins," *New York Times*, May 5, 2001, A1. Finally, in spring 2002, Pope John Paul II issued an apology for the clerical sex scandal that has rocked the Catholic Church. Melinda Henneberger, "Pope Offers Apology to Victims of Sex Abuse by Priests," *New York Times*, April 24, 2002, A1.

A very powerful argument that the Catholic Church still has not come to terms with its role in the Holocaust is the subject of Daniel Jonah Goldhagen's book *Moral Reckoning: The Role of the Catholic Church in the Holocaust and Its Unfulfilled Duty of Repair* (New York: Alfred A. Knopf, 2002).

4. "Hartford Courant Apologizes for Sale Ads It Published in Slavery Era," *New York Times*, July 6, 2000, A1.

5. See, for example, Ronald Steel, "Sorry about That," *New Republic*, April 20, 1998, 9; James Bowman, "Sorry about That," *New Criterion* (May 1998): 50; John Leo, "So Who's Sorry Now: History Is Packed with Shameful Occurrences. Where Will Group Apologies End?" *U.S. News & World Report*, June 30, 1997, 25; Richard John Neuhaus, "Apologies on the Cheap," *First Things: A Monthly Journal of Religion and Public Life* (April 1998): 82.

6. During his speech in Uganda in March 1998 (see note 14), President Clinton also made some general statements with respect to the institution of slavery: "And . . . going back in time before we were a nation, European Americans received the fruits of the slave trade. And we were wrong in that, as well."

7. See note 2.

8. The reference is to President Clinton's apology in Guatemala (see note 15). It is important to note that the president himself never made reference to genocide. However, he was responding to, and essentially affirming the findings of, an independent Guatemalan truth commission that had found the United States guilty of complicity in the genocide of the Guatemalan government. Mireya Navarro, "Guatemalan Army Waged 'Genocide,' New Report Finds," *New York Times*, February 26, 1999, A1.

9. There have been other efforts that do not rise to the level of a "state apology." For example, on September 8, 2000, the head of the Bureau of Indian Affairs formally apologized for the agency's participation in the "ethnic cleansing" of western tribes. Remarks of Kevin Gover, Assistant Secretary–Indian Affairs, Department of the Interior, at the Ceremony Acknowledging the 175th Anniversary of the Establishment of the Bureau of Indian Affairs, September 8, 2000, www.cet.nau.edu/Projects/ITEP/news/gover_remarks.htm [accessed April 22, 2004].

An example of a near apology would be Secretary of State Madeleine Albright's acknowledgment of various errors made by the United States in its relations with Iran. David E. Sanger, "U.S. Ending a Few of the Sanctions Imposed on Iran," *New York Times*, March 18, 2000, A1.

10. For an excellent treatment of this, see *When Sorry Isn't Enough: The Controversy over Apologies and Reparations for Human Injustices*, ed. Roy L. Brooks (New York: NYU Press, 1999), sec. 4.

11. Barkan, *The Guilt of Nations*, chap. 9.

12. It should be noted that the apology was delivered after a number of very large anti-American demonstrations were held in Athens. Hugh Stanley, "Huge March in Athens Protests Visit by Clinton," *New York Times*, November 18, 1999, A12; Marc Lacey, "President's Visit to Greece Yields a Toast and a Tumult," *New York Times*, November 20, 1999, A5. The apology was as follows:

When the junta took over in 1967 . . . the United States allowed its interests in prosecuting the cold war to prevail over its interests—I should say its obligation—to support democracy, which was, after all, the cause for which we fought the cold war. It is important that we acknowledge that.

13. The apology was delivered during a tour through several African states in spring 1998:

The international community, together with nations in Africa, must bear its share of responsibility for this tragedy, as well. We did not act quickly enough after the killing began. We should not have allowed the refugee camps to become safe havens for the killers. We did not immediately call these crimes by their rightful name: genocide. We cannot change the past. But we can and must do everything in our power to help you build a future without fear, and full of hope.

President Bill Clinton, *Remarks by the President to Genocide Survivors, Assistance Workers, and U.S. and Rwanda Government Officials*, Kigali Airport, Kigali, Rwanda, March 25, 1998, The White House, Office of the Press Secretary, http://clinton4.nara.gov/Africa/19980325 -16872.html [accessed April 22, 2004].

14. The apology was as follows:

It is as well not to dwell too much on the past, but I think it is worth pointing out that the United States has not always done the right thing by Africa. In our own time, during the Cold War, when we were so concerned about being in competition with the Soviet Union, very often we dealt with countries in Africa and in other parts of the world based more on how they stood in the struggle between the United States and the Soviet Union than how they stood in the struggle for their own people's aspirations to live up to the fullest of their God-given abilities.

President Bill Clinton, *Remarks by the President to the Community of Kisowera School*, Mokono, Uganda, March 28, 1998, The White House, Office of the Press Secretary (Kampala, Uganda) http://clinton4.nara .gov/textonly/Africa/19980324-3374.html [accessed April 22, 2004].

15. President Bill Clinton, *Remarks by the President in Roundtable Discussion on Peace Efforts*, National Palace of Culture, Guatemala City, Guatemala, March 10, 1999, The White House, Office of the Press Secretary (Guatemala City, Guatemala), www.fas.org/irp/news/1999/ 03/990310-wh1.htm [accessed April 22, 2004].

16. Susanne Jonas, "Dangerous Liaisons: The U.S. in Guatemala," *Foreign Policy* 103 (1996): 144–60.

17. John M. Broder, "Clinton Offers His Apologies to Guatemala," *New York Times*, March 11, 1999, A1.

18. John M. Broder, "Clinton Apologizes for U.S. Support of Guatemalan Rightists," *New York Times*, March 11, 1999, A12.

19. There were no stories reported from Central America on March 10, 1999, the day that the apology was issued, according to the Television News Archive at Vanderbilt University, http://tvnews.vanderbilt .edu [accessed April 22, 2004]. On March 11, CBS news correspondent Bill Plante filed a report from Guatemala City, but it concerned Clinton's defense into allegations of security leaks that allowed military secrets to go to China. The only story dealing with human rights in Guatemala was filed by CNN reporter Harris Whitbeck.

20. In all likelihood, the vast majority of the American public would not know even the most rudimentary facts of the U.S. government's involvement in Guatemala. In a seminal study conducted more than half a century ago, Martin Kreisberg categorized the American public's knowledge (or lack thereof, which he termed "dark areas of ignorance") of international affairs as follows: 30 percent of the population is unaware of almost any event in U.S. foreign affairs; 45 percent is aware of important events but cannot be considered informed; and 25 percent consistently shows knowledge of foreign problems. Martin Kreisberg, "Dark Areas of Ignorance" in *Public Opinion and Foreign Policy*, ed. Lester Markel (New York: Council on Foreign Relations, 1949), 51. More specifically, a number of studies conducted during the 1980s also give very strong evidence that the American public would have virtually no knowledge of U.S. involvement in Central America. See, generally, Miroslav Nincic, *Democracy and Foreign Policy* (New York: Columbia University Press, 1992), 28; Ronald Hinckley, *People, Polls, and Policymakers: American Public Opinion and National Security* (New York: Lexington Books, 1992), 80.

21. The U.S. Public Health Service's "Tuskegee Study of Untreated Syphilis in the Negro Male" represents an infamous chapter in the annals of American medical research. Starting in 1932, health researchers recruited 399 indigent Southern black men who were led to believe they would receive free medical treatment for what they called "bad blood." In fact, no such treatment was given, and while the researchers carefully monitored the "study," the disease claimed its victims. Alison Mitchell, "Survivors of Tuskegee Study Get Apology from Clinton," *New York Times*, May 17, 1997, A10. Clinton's remarks indicated some understanding of the wider ramifications of the study:

> The legacy of the study at Tuskegee has reached far and deep, in ways that hurt our progress and divide our nation. We cannot be one America when a whole segment of our nation has no trust in

America. An apology is the first step, and we take it with a commitment to rebuild that broken trust. We can begin by making sure
there is never again another episode like this one. We need to do
more to ensure that medical research practices are sound and
ethical, and that the researchers work more closely with communities.

President Bill Clinton, *Remarks by The President in Apology for Study
Done in Tuskegee*, The White House, Office of the Press Secretary,
May 16, 1997, http://clinton4.nara.gov/textonly/New/Remarks/
Fri/19970516-898.html [accessed April 22, 2004].

22. Mitchell, "Survivors of Tuskegee Study Get Apology from Clinton," A10.

23. In his political memoirs Brandt described his unexpected
actions:

I had not planned anything, but I had left Wilanow Castle, where
I was staying, with a feeling that I must express the exceptional
significance of the ghetto memorial. From the bottom of the abyss
of German history, under the burden of millions of victims of murder, I did what human beings do when speech fails them.

Even twenty years later, I cannot say more than the reporter
whose account ran: "Then he who does not need to kneel knelt,
on behalf of all who do need to kneel but do not—because they
dare not, or cannot, or cannot dare to kneel."

Willy Brandt, *My Life in Politics* (New York: Viking, 1992), 200.

24. See, generally, Stephen Schlesinger and Stephen Kinzer, *Bitter
Fruit: The Untold Story of the American Coup in Guatemala* (Garden
City, NY: Doubleday, 1982), 65.

25. The effort to remove Jacobo Arbenz began in early 1953, as the
CIA initiated contact with Guatemalan exiles under the leadership of
Carlos Acastillo Armas and began providing funds for training, equipment, and payment of a mercenary force. The pretext for overt American action occurred with the discovery of a small cache of Czech arms
on the Swedish ship *Alfhem*. On June 18, 1954, "Operation Success"
opened when Acastillo's mercenary army launched an invasion from
Honduras. To the surprise of American analysts, however, no popular
uprising took place. Because of this, CIA operatives were forced to take
a far more active role than what had been planned for, as agents began
regular bombardments of the capital and other cities. Susanne Jonas,
The Battle for Guatemala: Rebels, Death Squads, and U.S. Power (Boulder, CO: Westview Press, 1991), 29–30.

26. Jonas, *The Battle for Guatemala*, 42.

27. Formal U.S. counterinsurgency began as early as 1960, and U.S. Special Forces set up a secret military training base in Guatemala in 1962. Jonas, *The Battle for Guatemala*, 69.

28. Jonas writes: "U.S. training, bomber planes, napalm, radar detection devices and other sophisticated technology . . . were decisive in smashing the insurgency." Jonas, *The Battle for Guatemala*, 70.

29. On March 30, 1995, Clinton directed the Intelligence Oversight Board (IOB) to conduct a government-wide review concerning U.S. intelligence activity in Guatemala. On June 28, 1996, the IOB issued its report, which found that in attempting to achieve U.S. national security objectives in Guatemala, the "CIA dealt with some unsavory groups and individuals. The human rights record of the Guatemalan security services were [sic] widely known to be reprehensible, and although the CIA made some efforts to improve the conduct of the services, probably with some limited success, egregious human rights abuses did not stop." Anthony S. Harrington, *Report on Guatemala Review*, Intelligence Oversight Board, June 28, 1996, 1. The report continues:

> [W]e found that several CIA assets were credibly alleged to have ordered, planned, or participated in serious human rights violations such as assassination, extrajudicial execution, torture, or kidnapping while they were assets—and that the CIA Directorate of Operations (DO) headquarters was aware at the time of the allegations.

Harrington, *Report on Guatemala Review*, 3.

30. Anthony DePalma, "Canada's Indigenous Tribes Receive Formal Apology," *New York Times*, January 8, 1998, A3.

31. See note 15.

32. Harrington, *Report on Guatemala Review*, 3.

33. This is referencing at least two charges. The first relates to the consolidated suit *Xuncax v. Gramajo* and *Ortiz v. Gramajo*, 866 F. Supp. 162 (D. Mass., 1995). Xuncax and eight other Guatemalan citizens brought suit against Gramajo, the former defense minister of Guatemala, under the Alien Tort Statute, while Ortiz, a U.S. citizen, brought suit under the Torture Victim Protection Act. In her suit Ortiz claimed that while she was raped and tortured by Guatemalan security agents, a man she believed to be an American came in, cursed her tormentors, and told them to leave her alone because she was a U.S. citizen and because her abduction had been given wide coverage on the news. The man then drove her away in his car. During the course of this ride, Ortiz jumped out while they were stopped in traffic, and within forty-eight hours she had departed Guatemala.

The second reference comes from the lawsuit of Jennifer Harbury discussed in chapter 2. In addition to her "access to court" claim, Harbury also maintained that American officials had actively participated in the torture and killing of her husband, Guatemalan national Efrain Bamaca-Velasquez. The Court of Appeals for the District of Columbia allowed the "access" part of her suit to proceed, but threw out the claim of U.S. involvement on the grounds that even if American agents had participated in committing such atrocities, they did so beyond the borders of the United States.

34. Clifford Krauss, "How U.S. Actions Helped Hide Salvador Human Rights Abuses," *New York Times*, March 21, 1993, A1; Clifford Krauss, "U.S. Aware of Killings, Working with Salvador's Rightists, Papers Suggest," *New York Times*, November 9, 1993, A4; Tim Weiner, "Documents Assert U.S. Trained Salvadorans Tied to Death Squads," *New York Times*, December 14, 1993, A1.

35. J. M. Coetzee's Booker Prize–winning novel *Disgrace* deals with the issue of apologies and forgiveness through fiction. Although never mentioned, the background for the book is South Africa's Truth and Reconciliation Commission. In one of the most dramatic scenes in the book, the protagonist offers an apology to the father of a student he has had an illicit affair with, for which he has been dismissed from his university position. The father answers: "But I say to myself, we are all sorry when we are found out. Then we are very sorry. The question is not, are we sorry? The question is, what lesson have we learned? The question is, what are we going to do now that we are sorry?" J. M. Coetzee, *Disgrace* (New York: Viking, 1999), 172.

36. Elie Wiesel made this point during a ceremony for the dedication of a Holocaust remembrance site next to the Brandenburg Gate. According to a *New York Times* report:

> Mr. Wiesel concluded by urging Parliament to pass a resolution formally requesting, in the name of Germany, the forgiveness of the Jewish people for the crimes of Hitler. "Do it publicly," he said. "Ask the Jewish people to forgive Germany for what the Third Reich had done in Germany's name. Do it, and the significance of this day will acquire a higher level. Do it, for we desperately want to have hope for this new century."

Roger Cohen, "Wiesel Urges Germany to Ask Forgiveness," *New York Times*, January 28, 2000, A3.

37. See, generally, John Tirman, *Spoils of War: The Human Costs of America's Arms Trade* (New York: The Free Press, 1997).

38. Marc Lacey, "On Visit, Clinton Nudges Turkey on Rights," *New York Times*, November 16, 1999, A6.

39. As Mark Cocker has pointed out, the conquest of indigenous peoples was in large part premised on the "perfectability" of mankind, which meant that human progress was ostensibly being carried out through the elimination of "inferior" races. Mark Cocker, *Rivers of Blood, Rivers of Gold: Europe's Conquest of Indigenous Peoples* (New York: Grove Press, 1998).

NOTES TO CHAPTER 7

1. Sheryl Gay Stolberg, "U.S. AIDS Research Abroad Sets Off Outcry over Ethics," *New York Times*, September 18, 1997, A1.
2. Howard French, "AIDS Research in Africa: Juggling Risks and Hopes," *New York Times*, October 9, 1997, A1.
3. Sheryl Stolberg, "Use of Placebo Is Ended for H.I.V. Study in Africa," *New York Times*, October 24, 1997, A12.
4. Although the federal government's AIDS Drug Assistance Program was intended to provide AIDS drugs for everyone living in this country who was afflicted with the disease, long waiting lines for this medicine now threaten this national commitment. Esther Kaplan, "Dying for AIDS Drugs," *Nation*, November 3, 2003, 5.
5. Donald G. McNeil Jr., "Indian Drug Company Offers to Supply AIDS Drugs at Low Cost in Africa," *New York Times*, February 7, 2001, A1.
6. Rachel Swarns, "Drug Makers Drop South Africa Suit over AIDS Medicine," *New York Times*, April 20, 2001, A1.
7. Barbara Crossette, "A Wider War on AIDS in Africa and Asia: Experts Say That Cheaper Drug Treatments Alone Are Not Enough," *New York Times*, April 30, 2001, A6.
8. "Text of President Bush's 2003 State of the Union Message to Congress," *New York Times*, January 29, 2003, A12.
9. This is not meant to suggest that all has gone well. For one thing, rather than committing $3 billion for the first year as previously promised, the Bush administration has only proposed an additional $2 billion. In addition, rather than pumping this desperately needed money into the already existing Global Fund, the Bush administration has continued to insist that the money be spent through U.S. channels. Editorial, "Betraying the Sick in Africa," *New York Times*, September 4, 2003, A22; Donald G. McNeil Jr., "Plan to Fight AIDS Overseas Is Foundering," *New York Times*, March 28, 2004, A1.
10. It is difficult to discern moral standards from public opinion polls, and this particular issue is no exception. A poll conducted by the

Washington Post during the summer of 2002 indicates that there are tremendous levels of public ambivalence on this issue. For example, 74 percent of the respondents approved of Bush's proposal to spend what at that time was an additional $500 million over the next few years to help combat the transmission of the AIDS virus from mothers to unborn children. However, there was no overall support for otherwise increasing the U.S. commitment, with 47 percent doubting that additional assistance would lead to meaningful progress and 40 percent saying that it would. What was not surprising was that a much higher percentage of blacks (47 percent) ranked AIDS as the most urgent health problem than did whites (30 percent) or Latinos (37 percent). Finally, the public expressed harsh criticism of Africans themselves, with eight out of ten respondents saying that AIDS is the problem that it is in Africa because of the "unwillingness of people to change their unsafe sexual practices." Richard Morin and Claudia Deane, "Americans on AIDS in Africa: Help and Discipline Needed," *Washington Post*, July 6, 2002, A3.

11. Paul G. Harris and Patricia Siplon, "International Obligation and HIV/AIDS," *Ethics & International Affairs* 15 (2001): 29–52.

12. Sheryl Gay Stolberg, "Unlikely Coalition Stirs Congress in AIDS Battle," *New York Times*, May 12, 2002, A1.

13. Christian Barry and Kate Raworth, "Access to Medicines and the Rhetoric of Responsibility," *Ethics & International Affairs* 16 (2002): 57–70.

14. The availability of AIDS medicine has had some stunning effects. In one study in South Africa where AIDS medicine was provided free, within three months the virus was undetectable in 90 percent of the patients. Rachel L. Swarns, "Free AIDS Drugs in Africa Offer Dose of Life," *New York Times*, February 8, 2003, A1.

15. Bob Herbert, "Refusing to Save Africa," *New York Times*, June 11, 2001, A17. Ironically enough, perhaps, patients in Africa have been better at following their pill regimen than American patients. Donald G. McNeil Jr., "Africans Outdo U.S. Patients in Following AIDS Therapy," *New York Times*, September 3, 2003, A1.

16. Michael Ignatieff has captured both the maddening and the self-serving nature of Western "conscience" in this description of the West's failure to intervene in Bosnia:

> What needs to be understood more clearly—however pessimistic the implications—is that when conscience is the only linkage between rich and poor, North and South, zones of safety and zones of danger, it is a weak link indeed. If the cause of Bosnia

failed to arouse the universal outrage and anguish that the atrocity footage on our television screens led one to expect, it was not
because those watching such images in the comfort of their living
rooms lacked ordinary human pity. The charitable response was
quite strong. The real impediment to sustained solidarity ran
deeper: in some deeply ingrained feeling that "their" security and
"ours" are indeed divisible; that their fate and ours are indeed severed, by history, fortune, and good luck; and that if we owe them
our pity, we do not share their fate. Most of us persist in the belief
that while the fires far away are terrible things, we can keep them
from our doors, and that while they may consume the roofs of our
neighbors, the sparks will never leap to our own.

Michael Ignatieff, *The Warrior's Honor: Ethnic War and the Modern Conscience* (New York: Henry Holt, 1997), 108.

17. See generally, David Scheffer, "Toward a Modern Doctrine of
Humanitarian Intervention," *University of Toledo Law Review* 23
(1992): 253–93.

18. The standard list for humanitarian interventions prior to 1970 is
extraordinarily short: (1) Greece 1827–1830: Great Britain, France,
and Russia intervened in the Greco–Turkish War; (2) Syria 1860–1861:
Turkish rule led to the massacre of thousands of Maronite Christians
leading to French intervention; (3) Bosnia, Herzegovina, and Bulgaria,
1877–1878: Turkish treatment of Christian populations resulted in
Russia declaring war on Turkey with the consent of Austria, Prussia,
France, and Italy; (4) Macedonia, 1903: Turkish atrocities against civilian populations led to a declaration of war by Greece, Bulgaria, and
Serbia.

There have not been very many examples of humanitarian intervention in modern times either. Three of the more noteworthy interventions occurred in the 1970s, although not all international law scholars
would agree on whether these were "humanitarian" or not. In 1971
India invaded Pakistan after violence in East Pakistan (now Bangladesh) resulted in the deaths of tens of thousands and the creation of
ten million Pakistani refugees in India. That same year, Tanzania
invaded Uganda and had the barbarous Idi Amin removed from office.
And finally, in 1978 Vietnam intervened in Cambodia and pushed the
Khmer Rouge leadership out of the country. See, generally, Ved Nanda,
"Tragedies in Northern Iraq, Liberia, Yugoslavia, and Haiti—Revisiting
the Validity of Humanitarian Intervention under International Law—
part I," *Denver Journal of International Law and Policy* 20 (1992): 205–
334.

19. Article 39 reads: "The Security Council shall determine the existence of any threats to the peace, breach of the peace, or act of aggression and shall make recommendations or decide what measures shall be taken in accordance with Articles 41 and 42, to maintain or restore international peace and security."

20. For any number of examples of this response to genocide from policymakers, see Samantha Power, "*A Problem from Hell": America and the Age of Genocide* (New York: Basic Books, 2002).

21. The NATO intervention in Kosovo in 1999 was undertaken without Security Council approval, and one of the debates that has been going on since that time is whether Security Council approval is necessary under international law.

22. For an excellent treatment of this, see Walter Clark and Jeffrey Herbst, "Somalia and the Future of Humanitarian Intervention," *Foreign Affairs* (March/April 1996): 70–85.

23. David Malin Roodman, *Still Waiting for the Jubilee: Pragmatic Solutions for the Third World Debt Crisis* (Washington, DC: Worldwatch Institute, 2001).

24. Oxfam, "Rigged Rules and Double Standards: Trade, Globalisation and the Fight against Poverty" www.maketradefair.com/en/index .php?file = 03042002121618.htm [accessed April 22, 2004]. Edmund L. Andrews, "Rich Nations Criticized for Barriers to Trade," *New York Times*, September 20, 2002, A7.

25. For an excellent account of this case, see Richard L. Wilson, "Prosecuting Pinochet: International Crimes in Spanish Domestic Law," *Human Rights Quarterly* 21 (1999): 927–79.

26. Under Article 17 of the Rome Statute, the ICC shall determine that a case is inadmissible where:

(a) The case is being investigated or prosecuted by a State which has jurisdiction over it, unless the State is unwilling or unable genuinely to carry out the investigation or prosecution;

(b) The case has been investigated by a State which has jurisdiction over it and the State has decided not to prosecute the person concerned, unless the decision resulted from the unwillingness or inability of the State genuinely to prosecute;

(c) The person concerned had already been tried for the conduct which is the subject of the complaint . . . ;

(d) The case is not of sufficient gravity to justify further action by the Court.

27. Katarina Tomasevski, *Between Sanctions and Elections: Aid Donors and Their Human Rights Performance* (London: Pinter, 1997).

28. Joy Gordon, "A Peaceful, Silent, Deadly Remedy: The Ethics of Economic Sanctions," *Ethics & International Affairs* 13 (1992): 123–42.

29. For such a view, see David Cortright and George Lopez, *The Sanctions Decade: Assessing UN Strategies in the 1990s* (Boulder, CO: Lynne Rienner, 2000).

30. Ignatieff, *The Warrior's Honor*, 4–5.

31. In July 2001 a group of pharmaceutical companies agreed to slash the prices of five potent antituberculosis medicines in poor countries by up to 90 percent. "Cheaper Drugs for Resistant TB," *New York Times*, July 12, 2001, A6.

NOTES TO CONCLUSION

1. Henry Shue, "Exporting Hazards," *Ethics* 91 (1981): 579–606.

2. Having said this, what is essential is that we do not think of ourselves as the bastion of human rights protection. One of the most insightful critiques of the international human rights "regime" has come from Makau Mutua, who argues against what he calls the Savages–Victims–Savior syndrome under which Third World people play the role of both "Victim" and "Savage," while Western people get to play the role of the great humanitarian "Savior." Makau Mutua, "Savages, Victims, and Saviors: The Metaphor of Human Rights," *Harvard International Law Journal* 42 (2001): 201–45.

3. Quoted from page 5 of this book.

4. Joan Fitzpatrick, "Sovereignty, Territoriality, and the Rule of Law," *Hastings International and Comparative Law Review* 25 (2002): 303–40, 327.

5. "Text of President Bush's 2003 State of the Union Address to Congress," *New York Times*, January 29, 2003, A12.

6. "Text of President Bush's 2002 State of the Union Address to Congress," *New York Times*, January 30, 2002, A22.

7. Joseph Kahn, "U.S. Rejects Bid to Double Foreign Aid to Poor Lands," *New York Times*, January 29, 2002, A4.

8. President Bush's address to the United Nations on September 12, 2002, arguing in favor of military action against Iraq repeatedly made reference to Iraq's dismissal of international law. This from someone who removed the United States from the Kyoto Treaty, has vigorously fought against the creation of an International Criminal Court, and who single-handedly subverted the Anti-Ballistic Missile (ABM) Treaty.

9. Joseph Kahn, "Losing Faith: Globalization Proves Disappointing," *New York Times*, March 21, 2002, A6.

10. Elisabeth Bemuller, "Bush Plans to Raise Foreign Aid and Tie It to Reforms," *New York Times*, March 15, 2002, A8.

INDEX

Harris, Paul, 132
Hartford Courant, apology by, 117
H.B. Fuller Company, 23, 25. *See
also* Resistol (glue)
Heavily Indebted Poor Countries
initiative, 136
Hitchens, Christopher, 102
Holmes, Oliver Wendell, 21
Honduras: death squads in,
104–5; Nicaraguan Contras in,
104–5, 107; U.S. training site
in, 104
Howard, John, 176n1
humanitarian intervention, 134–
35, 188n18; in Bosnia, 135–36;
ethical/moral/legal interests
in, 135; by NATO in Kosovo,
189n21; noninterference versus, 135; in Rwanda, 136; in
Somalia, 135
humanity: inhumanity versus,
142; of other people, 147; in
ourselves, 147; recognition of,
142
human rights: abuses in El Salvador, 123–24; abuses in Guatemala, 123–24; abuses in
Honduras, 105; abuses in Turkey, 110; enforcing of, 136–37;
"ethical foreign policy" versus,
152n13; judgment of, 142
Human Rights Watch, 102
Human Rights Watch Arms Project, 168n6
human suffering: AIDS/diseases
and, 138; morality and, 138;
poverty and, 138; terrorism
and, 145–46; understanding
of, 146; U.S. ignoring of, 145
Hussein, Saddam, viii, 106
hypothetical scenario: extradition
treaty ignored in, 30; illegal

search in, 30; Rios as drug
kingpin in, 29–31, 33, 36–38,
41, 43

ICC. *See* International Criminal
Court
ICJ. *See* International Court of
Justice
Ignatieff, Michael, 138
Immigration and Nationality Act,
170n20
immoral actions, 146
Indonesia: communists elimi-
nated in, 105; Sukarno's
removal in, 105; U.S. support
of coup in, 105
INS v. Elias-Zacarias, 82
Intelligence Oversight Board
(IOB), 184n29
International Court of Justice
(ICJ), 63–64, 165n47
International Criminal Court
(ICC), 137, 163nn29–30,
190n8
International Criminal Tribunal
for Yugoslavia, 137
international law, 134–35
"International Obligation and
HIV/AIDS," 132
International Tribunal for
Rwanda, 137
intervention. *See* humanitarian
intervention
IOB. *See* Intelligence Oversight
Board
Iran: hostage situation relating to,
105–6; Mossadegh's removal
in, 105; Shah's regime in, 105
Iraq, viii; gassing of civilians in,
106; Hussein's regime in, 106;
Iraq–Iran War in, 106; U.S. eco-
nomic sanctions of, 106

ABOUT THE AUTHOR

Mark Gibney is the Belk Distinguished Professor at the University of North Carolina-Asheville, where he has taught since 1998. His publications have appeared in such journals as *Human Rights Quarterly, Harvard Human Rights Journal, Fletcher Forum of World Affairs, Boston College International & Comparative Law Journal, Georgetown Immigration Law Journal, Peace Review,* and the *Harvard International Journal of Press/Politics.* Previous books include the edited collections: *Open Borders? Closed Societies?: The Ethical and Political Issues* (1988); *World Justice?: U.S. Courts and International Human Rights* (1991); *Judicial Protection of Human Rights: Myth or Reality?* (1999); and *Problems of Protection: The UNHCR and Refugees at the Beginning of the 21st Century* (2003).